# IF STRENGTH HAD A *Price* I WOULD BE A *Millionaire*

## GALE *Johnson*

**LAMAR & LANORE**
PUBLISHING GROUP

# ACKNOWLEDGEMENT

**I WANT TO** thank God for my blessings. When I thought everything was coming down on me, you were there to give me the strength to keep going.

To my Mom and Dad (RIP), thank you for being there for me when I needed you the most. Thank you for helping me through all the tough times in life and for being such wonderful parents no matter what I did. Most of all, I thank you guys for being you. I will continue to make y'all proud.

To my sisters, thank you for always standing by me and to my son, Anthony Luis Martinez, whom I love so much for always understanding and loving me unconditional, I love you more than life. To Damon thank you for being a friend, thank you for being my lover and thank you for being my husband. You listen with a open mind never criticizing or scolding you share the good times and the bad with love and kindness, we have a bond between two souls not described by mere words. To my friends and fans, there is no more pleasing exercise of the mind than gratitude. It is accompanied by an inward satisfaction that the duties are sufficiently rewarded by the performance.

It is amazing how two words can mean so much. I appreciate all the love and support.

**THANK YOU,**

**GALE BLAZZE JOHNSON**

# DEDICATION

**I WOULD LIKE** to dedicate this book to Keisha and Sharon Johnson for always being loving sisters, mother figures, and most importantly my best friends. Life holds so many simple blessings, and that is exactly what you guys are every day of my life.

The deepest principle in human nature is the craving to be appreciated, and that is how both of you have made me feel, every second, moment, and day of my life. You are very special not only to me but to many others. I always try not to look at my past because it made my future feel like it was not worth anything. But you, Keisha and Sharon, never made me feel like my future was meaningless.

You never factored in my problems; you helped me get over my past and urged me to keep going. You made me happier, stronger, and better as a person. I will always thank you for that. I love you guys.

**LOVE YOU ALWAYS.**

**YOUR SISTER,**

**GALE BLAZZE JOHNSON**

# TABLE OF CONTENTS

# INTRODUCTION
## My Wrong Decisions

I'VE LIVED IN a world full of not-good-enough of imperfections, bad choices, and violence. I always wanted to be a smart girl with an open mind, but instead, I became an easy girl and opened my legs. I was always opening my legs to the wrong men, who would then become foolish once I opened my heart. I guess it was my strong ego and confidence that caused me to make so many mistakes. It definitely wasn't my friends I always had a great support system. My friends and family kept me grounded and tried to direct me on the right path. But ultimately, I still kept making my own wrong decisions.

It's not that I never made any good decisions; I did, but always when no one was looking. I felt I had to portray this hard side of me for the world like a shield. I did this because my life was a mess before I was 25. I was young and dumb and enjoyed stealing cars, carrying guns, and selling drugs. The fact that I was a good person that can be forced to do wrong doesn't make me less good. However, it also doesn't make all my wrongdoings less wrong. I loved to hang with the boys; something about their grimy ways was fun to me. I was more interested in being one of the guys than wearing dresses. The fellas said I was just a guy in heels.

I'm from South End Marina Village, the hard streets of Bridgeport, CT; I loved it. The hood was my home. I never wanted to leave the projects. I got myself into all kinds of nonsense. I left home at fifteen and quit school before I was seventeen, had two children before I was twenty-five, and was abused by men and became homeless before I was twenty-six.

Before all that, I had a wonderful mother, beautiful sisters and brothers, and a nice apartment. It wasn't much, but it was ours. I just didn't want to listen to my parents, so I had my own agenda. I didn't always respect my mom and never really gave a damn about what my dad had to say. I just wanted to do what I wanted to do and never cared or realized how much I was hurting my own mother. How could I have been so selfish?

My mother was a single parent struggling to take care of four children, and I just added to her problems. I was selfish and put her through nothing but aggravation and hurt. I would say to her that having me was a mistake, and she would respond by saying I was out of control which I was. All I cared about was the streets. Eventually, I started to hate the life I was living but I didn't know what to do about it so I just kept on making the same mistakes.

As the years passed, I realized that I did not love or respect my-self. The beautiful smile that God blessed me with was drowning from abuse, hate, fear, pain, anger, and depression. My days and nights were full of screaming – at others and also at myself. I never felt like I was good enough. I was a total wreck, a hot mess. I needed a change but I didn't know how. The street life was too addicting; I had to have the drug dealers, the cars, the popularity, and of course the root of all evil: the money. Eventually, I learned that it was not worth it trying to keep up with the Joneses. This life was going to destroy me forever if I didn't change. Gale Blazze Johnson, yes, I'm your girl. Everything a pretty girl shouldn't do, I've done it; everything a pretty girl shouldn't say, I've said it; everywhere a pretty girl shouldn't go, I've been there. I wanted to live my life without boundaries and I was willing to do anything to keep it that way.

My life was a series of lies and deceit. I couldn't figure out if I was deceiving my family and friends or simply myself.

Growing up, I thought I had been through hell and back, but that was nothing compared to the speed bumps that were ahead of me. As I started to grow out of my old ways, God began to test my strength! But when I fell, I immediately got back up. When I'm rejected, I fight harder. When love hurt, I fought to make it feel good. My experiences have made me who I am. I have the strength of 10 men, the courage of a lion, and the heart of a saint. I have survived the unthinkable and will continue to fight for my life no matter what obstacles come my way. I am a survivor and have paid my dues. I am now taking my destiny in my own hands; I've earned it. I know I can weather any storm because If Strength Had a Price: I'd Be a Millionaire!

# Chapter 1:

# AWAKE

"I used to think of death as an actress leaving the stage long enough to change into costume. Then I could back up into the light as a new character. But I'm not an actress, and in life, I don't pretend."

**I WOKE UP** in the hospital with tubes in my nose, both wrists bandaged—my family around me. Then I remembered that I had tried to kill myself the previous day. I swallowed over 50 pills and ran a razor blade across my wrist. "Why am I still here? I want to be dead". Although I thought my defeat was final. I didn't know I could rise and become stronger after this. But we all know that death leaves a heartache that no one can heal. Yesterday morning, I remember the events that led me here.

I stayed at my mother's house after my daughter passed away two months ago cause I did not feel comfortable in my home. She was like my light and saved me from the darkness, and now I am afraid of the dark because she left me alone. I had many memories of her there.

My apartment design is like a train; each room connected where I had to go through my daughter's bedroom to get to my bedroom. Her toys and clothes were still everywhere. I could smell her scent as if she was still sitting on my lap. Her soul was in that place. I knew what my plans were when I tried to kill myself that evening, and for the past two months, I have been keeping everyone's spirits up from this tragedy. I felt I needed to make people happy. I thought being blunting numb to these kinds of things can help me make the days a little easier. But I am deeply saddened about my daughter's death when no one is around. Sooner or later, I knew I would break; a lot was going on inside of me. I couldn't believe she's gone. I wanted to be alone. I was tired of pretending that everything was fine. I could not shake the feeling that I was empty and now lost. My whole world has turned upside down, and I could not figure out how to turn it back around. I didn't want to talk to anyone; I couldn't eat or sleep; essentially, every night felt like a nightmare. I just wanted to explode. I kept pacing around the house to figure out what I could do to make myself feel better.

They say destiny has two ways of crushing us: either refusing our wishes or fulfilling them, and I knew there was nothing else I wanted but for God to give me my daughter back. That was a wish that I knew was never going to be fulfilled. As I walked into my mother's room, I saw that her purse was on the bed with a Walgreens bag full of her newly refilled prescriptions. I said to myself; I don't have the strength to go on anymore. My heart can't hide the pain from the loss of my child. I can't keep this phony smile on my face nor comfort those who also loved Shanice. I grabbed the pills out of my mother's purse, walked out the front door, and ran into the street without any regard for the cars that were speeding by. I didn't care if they hit me. That would have just sped up what I was about to do. Knowing that I parked my car outside my mother's house, I had to walk about eight blocks until I reached my apartment. I went inside, closed the door, and stood there for a moment. Shanice's memories were so much. I slide down to the floor started crying, pulling my hair and banging my head against the door. Fighting death is challenging. He's a formidable opponent to defeat, and the only question I asked was, "why?" I have no answer yet. I seemed to be talking to myself—like a conversation that lasted for hours without an explanation. Not one day, hour, a minute, or second will ever stop me from loving or thinking about my daughter, just as parents of a living child unconditionally loving their children always and forever, so do us, bereaved parents. Is it wrong to want to say and hear her name just as much as non-bereaved parents do?

Suddenly, I jumped up and went to her room. I pulled all her clothes out of the closet, threw them out the window, ripped pictures off her walls, and smashed her toys. I was looking for anything that got in my way; I was grabbing dolls, games, and everything else that crossed my path; whatever couldn't go out the window, I threw out the door. I screamed in blind anger, screaming until my words are over. It felt like poison was eating away my insides. I just kept screaming, "Why? Why did this happen to me? To my daughter, my child, my baby, why? She didn't deserve this! God, tell me, what did I do to deserve this?" During the chaos, I grabbed the Walgreens bag on the floor. I tore it open, and inside we're all my mother's prescriptions. I snatched up all the bottles of pills and crawled into my bedroom.

I pulled myself up on the edge of the bed and sat there, simply looking at the pills in my hand. I popped open the first bottle and started taking them one at a time. It seemed like it was taking too long, so I popped two and then three until I looked down, and there were no more left. I hurled the bottle to the side and picked up the next one. The damn steroids are the same pills my daughter had to take for her asthma, but it was in liquid form. Those steroids made my daughter's hair fall out; she always had bald patches in her head, which I covered with ponytails and barrettes. The pills were tiny; I just poured them into my hand and chewed them up like they were candy. Then I threw the bottle against the wall and went for the next one in the bag. By the time I was able to open the top of the blood pressure pills, I had started to feel dizzy. Everything turned into a blur exactly where I wanted to be.

My cell phone suddenly rang. I had a feeling it was my mother or sister calling me. My mother's instincts were too on-point. I knew deep down inside she felt something was wrong with me because I'm that person in the family you'd call the life of the party. I was always cracking jokes or lifting someone's spirits. But that day at my mother's house, I was acting out of character. Plus, I knew she was probably on her way over, so I had to hurry this shit up. Now I'm tired of sealing the wounds of everyone else while mine is bleeding steadily. I had a box cutter blade on my dresser leftover when installing a new carpet in my bedroom a few weeks before. I grabbed it like a kid who just found her favorite toy and slid it straight across my wrist from one side to the other. Then I started to repeat the process on my other arm. The pills were doing their job because I had no fear of the pain; I really couldn't feel anything. My whole body had gone numb, and before I could finish slicing my other wrist, the entire room went black. The next thing I knew, I was in this hospital. The first thought I had was anger and resentment. I was so pissed that they had saved my life without asking for my permission.

I wanted to die, and they just violated my rights and my wish. I looked over at my mother, who was sitting right at my side. She looked like she hadn't slept all night. She was staring at my face; her eyes were red with dried tears. She said to me, with a cracked voice, "I was waiting for you to open your eyes. What were you thinking?"

I just rolled my eyes at her and turned my head the other way, hoping to stare at a blank wall. Instead, I'm looking into the eyes of my older sister, Sharon, and my boyfriend, Dee. The three of them were seated all around me. I guess I didn't make it clear enough that I did not want to be bothered. If I wanted to see someone, it would have been my sister Keisha, but she was not there. She was home with the kids. She is the only one in my family who always gave me the time of day to talk anytime. A few hours later, my mother and sister left, and Dee was in the hospital with me. He put his hands on me; I looked at him and saw his big brown eyes filled with tears. Could it be because of his love for me, or Dee felt sorry for me? I had never seen him cry before; I always thought Dee was tough.

Dee is 5'7 medium build, has a big bright smile, smooth talker with a short haircut. Everyone knew him; he was like a celebrity in the hood. The thing that attracted me the most was that he had money. The authentic rich guy of the hood, 9 to 5, you know, is not his thing. He is a straight street hustler. He looked me in the eye and said, "Girl, why are you doing this?" I looked at him and did not say a single word. "If your mother did not call me, you probably would have died," he choked out. "Your mother had a feeling that something was wrong. She noticed that you had been wandering around all day, and something in her spirit did not feel right. Then she noticed that you had gone, so she called me to look for your whereabouts. When we got to your apartment, we saw all of Shanice's belongings thrown out, so we ran upstairs to see what was going on. Luckily, there was an extra key because I was about to kick in the back door. When I went inside, we found you covered in blood. I did not know what to do. I thought I lost you. I took you in my arms and carried you to my truck. I jumped in the driver's seat and proceeded to the emergency room. It looked like a scene from a TV show ER; the doctor ran up to you and rushed you to the back. We have been waiting here all night for you to wake up".

I mumbled, "I take it that you never thought I would go out of my way to try and kill myself, but what if I didn't wake up?" I bet you would have been ok with that?" Then I just turned my head away from him. I didn't give a damn about anything he had to say to me. "What is wrong with you? Don't you want me to be here? He asked. I just pulled my hand out of his and waved him off in a motion to leave me alone. It's sad when the person you know becomes the person you knew, even though you are still staring right into their eyes when you can look past them like they were never a part of your life. Dee and I used to talk for hours, and now I cannot look at him. He was upset when I turned around, so he got up and left the room. I didn't care; I was drained and tired, and after a few minutes, I passed out. That is what I remember the most: darkness. The following two days, my family and Dee were in and out of the hospital to visit me, but I did not have the strength to talk to them. They ruined my plans. It takes a lifetime to live, but only a few moments to die. My memories of Shanice are lovely but also painful to remember.

The only thing I was tired of was my life: and sick of the people in it. There was nothing to save me from this hell—not even 50 pills and a razor blade. After a few days, three doctors came into my room. Two of them wore white jackets, and one just had on a shirt and tie. They looked like they were about to tell me when I was getting out of here. The doctor with the shirt and tie started to talk; he looked at me and said, "You are a fortunate young lady. Your family found you just in time. He went on to explain the treatments they did. "We had to stitch up both of your wrists and pump your stomach to clear you from all the pills you swallowed."

He assured me that I would be fine but that I would be a little sick from the medications they were giving me. I didn't care about that, so I snapped at him, "When do I get out of here?" He looked at me with compassion in his eyes and said, "You will not be going home just yet. We have to keep you here under observation for a while. So we will be taking you to the other side of the hospital into the psychiatric ward until we feel that you are safe enough to go home." I just lay there looking at them like they were crazy, even though the opposite was most likely the case. The doctors must have thought they were sending me where I needed to be. I know suicide doesn't change my circumstances. I was trying to eliminate the possibility of it getting any better.

# Chapter 2:

# INSANITY

"Sometimes we scream when everyone else whispers.
When I am trying to be heard, it is not for racket or distraction; it is because I am fighting for peace within me."

**A FEW HOURS** later, the doctor came back into the room, changed the bandages on my wrist, and removed me from all the tubes. A few minutes later, they helped me get out of bed and put me in a wheelchair. I wonder where they are taking me. They then wheeled me across the bridge that connects the regular hospital to the psychiatric ward of Bridgeport Hospital. My older sister Sharon, my sister Keisha and my boyfriend Dee came with me. Everyone crept in suspense of what was to come next. As we approached the double doors, they swung open, and a security guard was waiting to check me in alongside some nurses. He told Sharon, Keisha, and Dee that they had five minutes to say their goodbyes, for they will not be allowed to go beyond this point. I felt like I didn't have to be in a mental hospital to find my disordered mind. The world outside this place was already a mental institution. Sharon and Keisha grabbed me and hugged me tightly. They told me they loved me and will be back to see me tomorrow during visiting hours. I didn't even hug them back. I just sat there comatose, dazed off in another world. Dee grabbed me and kissed me. I just looked at him. After they said their goodbyes the nurses wheeled me through the double doors which were then shut tight and locked with my family standing there on the other side. I never felt so alone. The walls of this place were plain, shiny white. They wheeled me past a TV room off to my left and a nurse's station on my right, then straight ahead down the hall, there were many doors with little windows on them. One of the nurses wheeled me into the back of the nurse's station. She evaluated me, taking all my vitals. She was a pretty little nurse looking like she was in her mid-forties. After examining me, she wheeled me down to the room where I would be staying. The room did not have all the white walls and windows, and there were two single-sized beds on either side. There were no sheets or pillows on one of the beds, just a thin green, worn-out vinyl mattress. I'm guessing that was where I was supposed to sleep. I looked around the room, wondering where the hell my sheets and pillows were. Then the nurse told me she'd be right back to fix up my bed. "But don't get out of the wheelchair just yet," she warned me. So I just sat there, wondering what the hell came next. Shortly after, She came back with some sheets and prepared my bed. After that, she showed me around the ward. The first thing she showed me was the bathroom, straight across the hall. It looked like a high school bathroom, three toilet stalls, three sinks, and a big jailhouse mirror above. Then when we walked around the corner, where there was an open space with shower heads.

There were no curtains for privacy, just a drain on the floor and big liquid soap containers mounted on the walls. You got to be kidding me. After we left the bathroom the nurse walked me down to what looked like a lounge area where some of the patients were looking at the TV; a middle-aged white man sat Indian-style on the floor with Mannerisms like a child sitting next to him was a young lady she looked about twenty-two. The nurse let me know that she would be my roommate. There was another patient in the room sitting quietly. He was the only one who looked normal. He seemed young as well, somewhere around my age, and was sitting on the couch watching TV. Now and then, he would look around the room with a confused stare on his face at the other patients—kind of like what I was doing. The nurse let me know that everything we did there was on a schedule. She said we would wake up at 6 AM for our showers and medications; breakfast at 7, then group sessions at 11. We also had to be evaluated by the counselor daily, and lunch was strictly at noon, and so were visiting hours. If we wanted, we could have our family members come in and bring us food if we liked. But by 2 PM, all visitors had to leave and the patients had to attend another group meeting to discuss our issues. 5 PM was dinner time, and our visitors could return and stay until visiting hours were over at 8 PM.

When the nurse finished giving me the tour I went back to my room to lie down. I felt so uncomfortable; this was just abnormal for me. I lay there on that hard-ass mattress, looking up at those plain, white walls thinking when the hell I was going to get out of here. I just wanted to go home. My mind was racing; the last couple of years kept repeating in my head. I thought about my children's father and all the shit he put me through; then I thought about my daughter, my son, my parents, sisters, brothers, the fast life, and now – the crazy life. This shit was pure insanity. I wondered how to overcome this force of negative emotions, hatred, and anger and turn them into love and compassion for those who love me. Tears started to run down my face. I couldn't get my daughter out of my head. I kept seeing her face, hearing her voice, remembering how smart she was, and all the little funny things she used to say and do. I just missed everything about her; I never knew anything could hurt so much; loving someone is the world's most giving emotion. Even a happy life cannot be without a measure of darkness. I always say the word "happy" always loses its meaning if not balanced without suffering by our sadness. Out of nowhere, my roommate burst into the room and started yelling and screaming. She looked at my tear-stained face and ran over to me, yelling and pointing, "Why are you crying? I looked startled, not knowing what she was going to do next. The nurses ran into the room and yelled for her to stop. She kept yelling back at them, "No, my roommate is bothering me." The nurse replied, "She is not bothering you. Go back into the lounge and watch TV. They say, "Do not judge, or you too will be judged for the same way you judge others," but I couldn't help looking at her like she was just another lunatic. I didn't know what drove her to her madness and wasn't sure whether I should hit her or help her. I have never been through anything like this, but I told myself that every individual has a place in this world and that I have to respect this, whether I like it or not. I knew I had to figure out how the hell to get out of this crazy house. I wasn't psycho, just depressed, and to not sink my mind into more depression.

I walked down to the TV lounge where the rest of the patients were. Most of them seemed to be in the same positions they were in when I first arrived. I sat on the opposite end of the couch, where the only person besides the nurses looked and acted normal. He was watching some old movie, or more like the movie was watching him. He must have felt the same way I felt right about now. "Wanting to get the heck out of here," the guy sitting Indian-style on the floor, as he rocked back and forth, just smiling and pointing at the TV while the guy sitting on the couch with me did not budge. It was as if he didn't even notice I had entered the room. I couldn't go anywhere, and I damn sure was not going back in the room. By 9 PM, it was lights out, and all of us had to go back to our rooms. I walked in and saw that Millie was still sitting in her wheelchair, facing the door with her head leaned back. A few minutes later, one of the nurses came in and put her to bed. I just sat on the corner of the bed looked at her, waiting to see if she was going to jump up and start screaming at me again, praying to God she didn't because—she scares the shit out of me more than I have ever felt in my life. Even living in the projects felt safer than this. This place was worse than jail. It was straight insanity. I scooted up on the bed with my back against the wall and curled my legs to my chest as I wrapped my arms tightly around them and watched Millie like a hawk. I couldn't fall asleep with all these depressing thoughts clogging my mind. I just had to sit there and stare at the walls. By the time I felt myself drift off, I had heard the nurses coming up the halls, waking everybody up for our meds to escort us to the nurse's station, where we all had to line up and receive our medication. One by one, we were each given these little white cups filled with pills. Some only had to take one like me prescribed for depression others had to take more.

"Good morning, ladies. Time for your medicine," The nurse said in an annoyingly cheery voice. I didn't think there was anything to be so damn cheerful about in here. Millie rolled her head forward to face the nurse. My eyes watched her roll the cart over to Millie. She handed her one of the cups of meds and a small plastic cup of water. Millie grabbed the pills and swallowed them down like a pro. She stuck her tongue out at the nurse showing her that the drugs were gone. Then the nurse grabbed two more cups and headed over to me. "Damn," I breathed. "You have to take it." I just looked at her. I shot the pill in my mouth, quickly followed with a cup of water. She stared in my face waiting for me to open my mouth; it was mandatory to Make sure everyone swallowed their pills. "Wider," she replied. I just dropped my jaw. Two minutes later, she came back into our room and ordered us into the shower. Damn, I thought. Can't we do anything on our own time? I just inched myself back up on the bed and stayed there. I sat there staring out the entrance to make sure they were gone. Then I stuck my finger in my mouth to dig out the little white pill that fits securely in the hole of my back tooth. They were not going to have me all medicated up; that's how they turn you crazy. I did that every time they gave me my medication. I put that damn pill right in that hole in my tooth. The morning was ending, and it was time for lunch. My sisters, Keisha and Sharon, showed up to visit me, and Sharon even cooked my favorite meal. Honey glazed ham with macaroni and cheese. It was so lovely of her, but I wasn't in the mood to eat. We all just sat there staring at each other for a while. I didn't want them to feel bad, so I tried to force myself to take a bite of the food. I couldn't. I just pushed the plate away from me. Keisha spoke first.

"The doctor said they didn't know when they were going to release you."

Did they tell you anything?

"I looked at her. "

Then she stated. If you play crazy and don't talk to them, they will keep you in here longer and keep giving you meds as if you need them. I know you're hurting but believe it or not, you provide me with strength. "to be depressed is to be lonely, and you still have a beautiful little boy at home that misses his mommy." Maybe she's right about my son, but I wished she could put herself in my shoes. She would feel how bad this hurts. Keisha had been working in the hospital for years and knew all the ins and outs. I knew, too, I had been dealing with hospitals for so long in my life, I may as well have made it my second home. Especially with Shanice's illness, she had the most severe form of asthma, making the hospital our second home. My sisters kept trying to talk to me, and they see that I was not in the mood for conversation so they spent about 45 minutes trying to communicate casually with each other. Shortly after, they both decided to leave, letting me know they would be back the next day. Dee walked in minutes after they were gone. I wondered if he had run into them in the hallway. I caught his eye right away. He sat next to me at the table and put his hand on my knee.

"Are you all right today?"

I shook my head. No.

He just put his arm around me and gave me a big hug. He kissed my forehead. I didn't want him to let me go. I just rested there for a while, tears running down my face. He knew just what I needed. He didn't make any small talk, ask me any questions, or stare at me like a crazy person. He just held me to comfort me. He was always a sweet guy. Dee stayed until about an hour before visiting hours ended. He asked me if I would be OK again and told me he would see me tomorrow. I let him ease his arm from around me and get up to leave. As he started walking away from me, he turned around and said, "I love you." Love to me is a feeling that words cannot describe, but at that moment, it felt priceless. I watched him leave, all the way to the end of the hall, through the double doors. I was alone again, waiting to be taken back to my room with Millie. I didn't know how I was going to get through another night. Never have I dealt with anything more complex than my soul.

# Chapter 3:

# THERAPY

"Happiness is not the absence of conflict, but it is the ability to cope with it. The more we live, the more we understand that life is not a 50/50 proposition."

AFTER A FEW days of starving myself and not taking showers, I not only experienced death, but I smell like it. Keisha, Sharon, and Dee have been coming regularly at the same time for the past three days. Dee would stroll in minutes after Keisha and Sharon; it seemed as if they were on a schedule that they had discussed amongst each other ahead of time to make sure there was always someone there with me. My mother had also popped up the day before. My father or my brother Tee never visit me. I bet if my other brother Augie was still alive, I know he would be there every day to see me. We were real close. I miss him too. I'm surprised my mother didn't try to talk my ear off. She just sat there looking at me with this expression on her face, one of "where did I go wrong." I didn't care, though, because I would have let her know precisely all the many places she went wrong to get it off my chest. I didn't have to argue to get my mother started up potentially. She knew how to take it too far, and I wasn't in the mood. Honestly, I was getting tired of being here altogether. Keisha and my mother had kept reminding me that I needed to talk in the group meetings and the counseling sessions if I was ever going to have a chance of getting out of here. All I had done so far was stare at the walls when it was my time to visit my counselor. For some reason, he seemed content with that. After the first day, he introduced himself.

I stared; he asked me if I wanted to talk. I stare; he wrote something on his clipboard. I stared; And then he let me go, assuring me, "Whenever you're ready to talk, I'm all ears." And for some odd reason, Dee was strangely calm about me being in here. He would console me and visit me every day, but he wasn't giving me any encouraging feedback on getting out. Maybe Dee didn't know what to say. With all the things we had been through since we been together, he was probably trying to figure out a way to leave me without risking me jumping out of the fucking window. Shit, if his ass would have just left me there to die, none of us would be here in this damn hospital trying to figure out what to do next. I feel like I'm being tortured for my anger, flashbacks, memories, and floods of painful emotions, and would have been punished by my anger if I had died, and feel my family committed a crime against my suicide. But if it weren't for my sisters, I would be in here looking like Millie. They kept me sane. My sisters have always been my angels here on earth. I damn sure wouldn't be talking to anyone if they were not around. And I don't want them to hurt, so I know I have to figure a way to get out of this place. When the nurse came in for shower time, I jumped up off the cold green vinyl mattress. She looked at me, shocked at first, then smiled a little to show she approved that I was finally taking a shower. When we got into the bathroom, we had to take off all our clothes and walk into this ample space where everyone could see us. I stood under a shower spout and let the Luke warm water drench my body. I instantly felt like a part of the human race again. I closed My eyes and I imagined I was back at home in my bathroom where it was way better than this. I reached for the soap dispenser and filled my hands with that liquid until it poured over. I began to lather my entire body with that generic unscented soap all over my neck, shoulders, arms, and head. I was rubbing and scratching and cleaning fanatically. I just wanted to wash off all the shit that piled up on me from life. I just kept scrubbing and scrubbing and rinsing and scrubbing. Suddenly the shower became my favorite place in the crazy house. Just as I started to feel my body levitate, the nurse yelled out, "OK, ladies wrap it up, shower time is over." We walked over to the nurses in a single file, and they gave us these thin-ass white towels to dry our bodies off. Then they handed us a clean pair of hospital scrubs to dress in. Unfortunately, it was back to reality. But I couldn't wait until tomorrow to escape again. That shower was the most therapy I had since I had been in here. Only if that were all I had to do, I'd be out of here by the end of the week. It was time to return to the councilor's office. As I entered the room, I sat on the hard metal school chair, staring at the door and wondering why the hell they couldn't put a cozy chair in here. The furniture is half the reason people go crazy here. They can't offer us a piece of the natural world by giving us simple things like soft sheets and pillows or a comfy chair to relax in while we pour our hearts out to the doctors. James Smith – that was my counselor's name. I thought it sounded just like the name of a counselor or someone in that profession. He had the name of a doctor. James Smith, definitely someone you could trust in a confidentiality conversation. Or at least that's what it seemed. He must have noticed the difference in me instantly because he sat down in front of me and smiled. "You ready to talk today, Ms. Johnson?" I nodded my head slightly and slowly put my head down. "How are you feeling today?" he asked with genuine concern in his voice.

"Better," I mumbled.

"What is it about today that makes you feel better than yesterday?"

"I took a shower." James could not help himself because a smile lit his face up at my response.

"Well, that's a start," he commented.

"How did it make you feel when you took the shower?"

"It made me feel alive again."

"Has it been a long time since you've felt alive?"

"I haven't felt alive since before my daughter was born."

James arched his eyebrows up at me like he knew this was going to be a horror story. I just nodded my head to reassure him he didn't misunderstand what I said. "So where do you want to start?" "I guess as far back as I can remember, although that will take more than an hour because I can write a book on all the bullshit I've been through in my life." "Well, I am all ears," he said, staring intently into my eyes. I felt like he was going to burn a hole in my head with his penetrating gaze. I looked out into space and began thinking of my crazy life. Then my words just started flowing out like a river. It felt like this was something I had needed for a very long time. James just sat there with his mouth open in disbelief of what was coming out of my mouth. And I told him everything, from as far back as I could remember.

# Chapter 4:

# EXPOSED

"A mistake is an opportunity to learn from your situation, but a learning situation doesn't necessarily have to be a mistake."

I HAVE BEEN through so much in my life, and I am shocked that I am still standing. I think back to when I was young. I was very mannish and grown acting. My mother had no control over me. She would say to people, "Where did this child come from? I swear I think she was switched as a baby." I would reply, "From you. They say the apple don't fall far from the tree." She would laugh and tell me that I don't act like her but that I act just like my father. I was such a tomboy growing up. I would hang out with all the guys in my neighborhood. I stayed outside hanging around with the fellas. I never hung out with females too much; it just wasn't my thing at the time. The hood was all I've known, especially where I was from, South End Marina Village. Hell, I never wanted to leave the projects; that place was my world. I would get into all kinds of bullshit. Summertime was the best because everybody would be hanging out, doing absolutely nothing. That may sound crazy, but to us, it was fun. My mother was not having any of it, but I didn't give a damn. No matter how much she tried to keep me out of trouble, I was always into something. I was the youngest of my parents' four kids. I had two older sisters, Sharon, Keisha, and an older brother, Tee. My dad had other children from previous relationships, and one of them grew up with my family. His name was Augie. My dad's other children are much older than we are, but we are all very close. I guess you can say my pops was a rolling stone. But only three of us lived with my mom. My oldest sister Sharon lived in Marina Village also, but she stayed across the way with my Aunt Nita. We called her Aunt Neet for short. Since Sharon was a baby, my Aunt Neet would always spoil her and take care of her like she was her own. For no apparent reason, she just adored Sharon. Now my brother Tee, I wished he lived with someone else because he was nothing but trouble. He gave our mother straight hell and constantly tortured me and my sister Keisha. Tee would cut off our ponytails in our sleep, beat us up, set our beds on fire, rip the heads off of our dolls, and whatever else to see us cry. I always thought he was crazy. I hated growing up with him; he was just an out-of-control kid. He even got to the point where he would disrespect our mother, cursing her out, smoking cigarettes in front of her, and drinking. Tee thought he could do whatever he wanted at all times, but after a while, my mom got tired of his ass. She couldn't deal with him anymore, so she put him in a place called "Boys Village," a group home for out-of-control teen boys. Although our father was in our life, you might also say my mother was a single parent. She did everything on her own. Money was real tight. My father never lived with us or took care of us like a father was supposed to. From time to time, he would just come over and spend the night simply because he missed being bothered by my mom – if you know what I mean. It would make me so mad knowing he didn't do shit for us, but he felt like he could still just come around when he wanted to. After my mother had given him four children, she found out he was married. So I used to ask Keisha, "Why do mommy put up with his shit?" I guess "Self Respect" is a question of recognizing Whether or not everything you thought was worth having does have a price. We never understood. When we got low on cash, we would walk to my dad's job when it was almost time for him to get off work– most of the time, I would go by myself. He was working at a factory called Jenkins Valves. I would sit on top of the hood of his car in the parking lot when it was almost time for him to get off work and beg him for a few dollars. I could tell he used to hate when I did that shit, but I didn't care; we needed money, and he was always trying to avoid us. Most times, he would drink. That man stayed drunk, sometimes for days at a time. I didn't mind it because it was just an easy way for us to get money out of him without begging for it. After all, if my father was sober, there was no way in hell we would get more than a couple of dollars out of his ass. A lot of times, when he was intoxicated, I would steal his car keys. I didn't care if I got in trouble; it didn't matter to me; I just wanted to drive. I used to pick up some of the fellas and joy ride for hours. I was under-aged with no license. Half the time, my dad used to be so drunk I didn't have to steal his car keys. He would give them to me and tell me to take him places, like another woman's house or the nearest bootlegger, to buy more alcohol after hours. My mother never knew about me driving the car cause if she found out where we went, we both would have gotten our asses whooped.

Most of the time, I didn't care if I got the car or not because I and some of the guys I hung around with had a stolen car all the time. We did it to get around. That shit came in handy when we needed to make extra money hustling. We had a car almost every day; that's how I learned how to drive. One of my homeboy's name Rich taught me how to pop locks and drive them cars right out the parking lot. I was digging that shit; at the time, that was one of my homeboys for real. He and his brother Mark; I loved them growing up because they didn't give a fuck just like me. The only thing different about us is that I went to public school and they went to Catholic school. I used to laugh so hard. Because you would think with those uniforms that they had to wear, they were good kids. As soon as those khaki pants came off, it was the total opposite. But they were loyal guys. It used to be a bunch of us hanging out, getting into all kinds of dumb shit. My mother knew I was up to no good, but she could never prove it. She had already gone through hell with my brother Tee, and I was not making things any better for her. Keisha was always the quiet one. She was the good one. She never gave my mother any trouble at all. But me, on the other hand, was just one of the guys wilding out and being a knucklehead. I guess you can say I enjoyed nonsense. Hell, I didn't care. I had to get it by any means necessary because my mom never really had it. Don't get me wrong; she always tried to portray that we had it and that she was the best mom in the world, but we knew what was going on. I know nobody is perfect, but there were many times when our lights, phone, and gas got cut off. I mean, what was I supposed to do with no food and tiny clothes? Shit, we slacked on a lot of things plenty of times. There were times when we ate hotdogs for a month because that was all we had, but I never looked at my mother any different. I always loved her, no matter what. I did get frustrated about our different living situations many times, though. I was disrespectful, but I was doing half the crazy bullshit because we always lived without many things. "You seem like you have a lot of resentment towards your mother," Dr. James observed. "No, it's not that I resent her; I did not agree with all the decisions she made. I am not saying that she hasn't been the perfect mother, but there are things that I know that I would have done differently."

"Have you ever talked to her about how you feel?" he asked.

I laughed slightly. "When you say talk…does that include arguments?"

"No, it means to have you respectfully sit down with her and discussed how certain situations made you feel?

"Not that I can remember."

"What about your father? You ever talk to him?"

"No, as I said, he was never around much for us to have serious talks like that, and when he was, he was drunk."

James leaned back in his chair and crossed his legs in front of me. Then came a slight knock at the door – I could see the nurse's head peering through the glass. James signaled for her to come in. "Are you ready for the next patient?" she smiled. "Yes, give us a moment to wrap this up," he said pleasantly. The nurse quietly shut the door. James looked at me and said, "So, this was a good start, Ms. Johnson. We can pick up from where we left off tomorrow. Let's try to figure out how these events in your life led to your being in here." I rolled my eyes away from him and walked to the door. "See you tomorrow," James sang as I shut the door behind me.

# Chapter 5:
# GROUP HUG

"It seems like everything here is strange. Maybe
a person needs a little madness or else they would
never dare to cut the ropes to be free."

THESE DAMN MANDATORY group sessions are killing me. All I want to do
is cover my damn ears because listening to these people is just depressing. I cannot understand why the hell they even make us do this. Why
would they put a bunch of depressed people in one room and force
them to have a conversation? The only thing good about the meetings "over the cuckoo's nest" was that my cousin Tracy, who had been
a counselor in Bridgeport Hospital's psych ward for six years, ended
up leading our sessions. When I first saw her, I smiled. I knew she
would look out for me. I wouldn't have to pretend like I was opening
up to these lunatics or anything; she would make sure I got an excellent recommendation to get out of here no matter what. Everyone sat
in the TV lounge in a semi-circle. Most of the group spaced out while
Tracy gave her an overview of how the session would run. After she an-
nounced all the procedures, she went around the room asking everyone
to describe

"how you are feeling today."

I usually just said, "I'm fine," or "I'm getting better,"
then passed along the baton. I wasn't opening up to those people. Shit, it's not like I was trying to make friends in here. One person who did take advantage of her group time was Millie. She would take up her time telling all about how spirits are amongst us and how she has to stay safe from the doctors because they try to control her. I thought she might be crazy to myself, but she knew what the hell was going on here. She was right on-point with what the doctors were doing to her. Life challenges are not supposed to paralyze you; they are supposed to help you discover who you are. But I guess people with little under-standing are most apt to act the way they want when their senses are in question. They were giving her so much medication she was like a damn puppet. I felt sorry for her; that's why I continued to hide my pills in my tooth cavity. They weren't going to have me drugged the hell up, hearing voices. Even though I felt comfortable with Tracy lead-ing the sessions, I still wasn't opening up. I guess these sessions were supposed to help us cope with our problems and practice life outside of this place. Pain is a part of living, as they say. It does not last forever, nor is it unbearable if shared with others. On the other hand, I wasn't taught that, so in a way, these sessions helped. Frankly, though, I was getting sick of this place altogether. I just wanted to go home and try to figure out a way to pull my life back together. Another thing that was kind of good about these group sessions was that I kind of made a friend. His name was Rodger; he was in for trying to commit suicide like me. He was the guy I had seen earlier, watching TV; the only other normal-looking guy in here. He was about 5' 10, with brown skin and a friendly smile. We kept looking at each other from across the room, shock at how the nurses handling most of the patients. You would have thought some of the nurses were 300-pound linebackers, the way they jumped on the patients. Things are just too crazy around here. John—who is usually Millie's partner in crime (or at least they always play blocks and games together)—was sharing how he felt during his turn in the session. Millie was rocking back and forth, whispering to

herself – which is her usual routine when speaking. Out of nowhere, she jumped up and charged John. Roger was sitting next to John, so he had to jump out of the way. He hopped out of her path and almost knocked clean into the table. He shot a look over at me like, "This bitch is crazy." My eyes damn near jumped out of my head in shock at the craziness.

After everything settled down, I sat down next to Roger on the couch in front of the TV. He adjusted his eyes from the TV to me, flashing me a friendly smile. I smiled back. "What the hell have we got ourselves into?" He chuckled, "The madhouse." "I don't know how much more of this I can stomach," I confessed. "Me either. Shit, they should have just let me die if I knew they were going to lock me up with all these crazy people." "For real," I said to him. "I know what I was doing. No voice in my head told me to do what I did. Shit would have been just as hard for them if any of these doctors' children died. Then they can come to talk to me about how they feel. It is one of those things you don't wish on anyone, but if you experience it, you don't want to talk to nobody about it that has not gone through it." "Yeah. That has to be tough." "It is unbearable." "My situation is completely different." Roger put his head down to avoid eye contact, feeling ashamed of his attempt. "I just felt like there was nothing for me to contribute to this world. I'm not good at anything but selling drugs – and I served two bids for that, so I don't know how good at that I am. I dropped out of high school. I'm an alcoholic, no parents, and homeless…" He sighed. "I mean, what's my purpose?" Roger was seeking an interlude from emotional pain and searing his mental agony. "Well," I started, "God saved both of us, so I guess now he just needs to show us what our purpose is."

"I hope he shows me quick because once they let me out of here back onto the streets, I go. I don't know what I'm going to do… Do you?"

"Do I what?" I asked, giving myself time to think about the question that had not even crossed my mind since I've been here. "Do you know what you are going to do once you get out of here?" I sat silent for what seemed to be the longest minute in history. "I guess I'm going to go home with my sister and raise my son." Saying it out loud seemed to put everything into perspective. It was almost like I had forgotten I had another child. Not that I forgot, but, how could I try to kill myself knowing my baby's father is in jail, and that his sister just died? I would have actually added to his list of traumas, that his mother killed herself? As the words rung in my head I was consumed with so much guilt I felt like I was going to burst. It hit me like a bolt of lightning how much of a coward move that was. I could not shake the feeling. I need to learn how to get into the therapy that is associated with me, fight for myself, do not be distracted, and stop the devil from being too busy. God is the glue that holds my life and faith together. "You all right?" Roger's voice awoke me from my trance. I struggled out and said in a different voice, "Yeah, I'm all right." "You have the death stare on your face." "Isn't that a common face around here?" I joked, trying to shake the mood. "I guess it is." He laughed. Roger turned his head back to the TV and continued watching the repeat of Law and Order. After that conversation with Roger, I just mentally disappeared from that place. I felt so numb inside I didn't know if I was capable of moving anymore. What I did know, though, was that it was time for me to finally leave this place and get my life back on track and figure out a way to get my son back. I had to get over this. God had to put me here for a reason, and like Roger said, "I have to figure out my purpose.

# Chapter 6:

# GAME PLAN

"A beautiful life does not just happen; it is built daily by prayer
humility, and sacrifices."

JAMES MUST HAVE been startled as I bolted through the door of his office because his eyes were wide open, and he let out a loud gasp. For
the first time since I've been here, I got a good night's sleep. Millie got
shipped off to an actual mental asylum after that last attack on John.
They must have figured there was no cure for her here. She needed
some real mental attention. So, I had the room to myself. Right before
I drifted off into a deep, peaceful sleep, I had it all set in my head for
what I would do to make sure I got out of this place fast. My game
plan was to go into James's office and spill like a snitch. I decided I
would tell him every detail of my damn life so he can feel sorry for
me, knowing he could never survive what I've been through, and immediately give me a Get out of jail free card for having a hard life. He
would have to see that I am just a regular person who has been dealing
with some irregular situations. By the time our session finishes, he will
offer me back my 40 acres and a mule along with my recommendation
for release.

I plopped down in the hard metal chair, ready to talk. James looked at me, confused at my sudden enthusiasm and change of attitude. "You look much better today, Ms. Johnson." "I feel better." "What caused this change?" "For starters, I didn't have to sleep with one eye open since Millie was relocated." "That would make anyone sleep better." "Sure would." "Yesterday, we had a good session. You got some good sleep maybe if we have another good session today, you will get good sleep again tonight." "That is exactly what I plan on doing," I said, as a big smile spread across my face. "We left off yesterday with the relationship between you and your mother. Have you had any time to think about how that affected your life?" "I did think about it, and I can pinpoint a part of my life that really stands out that affected my relationship with my mother. It was when we moved out of the projects." After living half my life in Marina Village, my mom came to us one day and said we were moving. When we asked her why she told us because they raised her rent and didn't want to pay such a high rate in the projects, she said we could live somewhere better without all the shootings and drug dealers. She had a point, we couldn't argue with that, so we moved. But after we left the projects, shit got worse. We never stayed in one place for more than six months at a time. We lived from house to house for years, and with every different home came more financial problems. We were never stable, and I was trying to figure out my mother's downfall. She always kept a job, so it's not like we were on welfare. She was a school teacher for special education children for 26 years. She kept herself together no matter what she was going through; she always looked like a million bucks. I never saw my mother without high heels or nice clothes. Don't get me wrong; even though we slacked on many things, she kept her children well put together. That's one thing my mom did not play around with was her kids. Times were just hard. After my dad left, my mother had a few boyfriends. She never seemed to pick any good ones, though. When she first stopped dealing with my father, she started messing with this guy named Pete. He was this tall, skinny-ass man with glasses. We didn't like him. She had been dating him for a long time on and off, even when we lived in Marina Village. Pete was a no-good type of guy. He was the one who introduced my mother to cocaine. She fought with a cocaine addiction for a while; every time she would try to clean herself up, he would always come around and bring her back down. One night, Keisha, Tee (who was on a home visit from Boys Village), and I were in bed sleeping, and the fighting in the kitchen had awakened us up. When we ran downstairs, my mom had Pete's ass pined up against the washing machine, choking him half to death with his necktie. We were so scared, crying, "Mommy, please let him go! You're going to kill him!" His eyes were rolling into the back of his head. We thought he was dead. All I could think about was my mother going to jail for the rest of her life and that we would never see her again. Then my brother ran to our neighbor's house for help. Our neighbor's name was Ms. D. She had lived next door to us in the projects for years; she was like a grandmother to us. She called the police, then ran into our door, trying to help calm my mother down. But no one could pull my mother off of Pete's neck. Finally, our neighbor's son somehow unraveled my mother's hands from his necktie. Pete fell limply onto the floor from my mother's grip, gasping for air and grabbing at his throat. He bumped his head against the washing machine as he went down. The cops came running in like there was a murder. My mother and Pete were all bloody, and we were all crying and screaming because we were scared. The cops started asking everyone questions. Pete just jumped up and ran out of the house holding his neck. I don't know if he went to the hospital or not, but we realized that the blood on the floor was his blood. The cops just took everyone's statement and left. They were nice since Pete didn't stick around to press charges. They just took the report and left. We didn't see Pete for weeks so I thought their relationship was over. Then by the end of the month his ass was back in the house acting like nothing ever happened. He knew we didn't like him but we held it together because of our mother. The truth is we wanted him gone. The first place we moved to after we left Marina Village was a house not too far away, only about 10 minutes on Iranistan Avenue.

It was a beautiful house; it reminded me of the Cosby Show, the way they did it, as you could go up the stairs from the kitchen or the living room. Keisha and I shared a room, just like we did when we were in the projects. Like all things "too good to be true," the house was no different. We started seeing mice droppings all over the place. It was on the counters, under the tables, in the corners of the wall, basically all over the house. One day we finally saw a mouse. Then there were two, then three, then a whole football team of them. I felt like I was sleeping in the subways in New York City. It got so bad they would crawl in the bed with us. They would run up our curtains and even come out of the light sockets as tiny newborns. The newborns were slimy and pink – OH my God, it was disgusting. It got to the point where we would huddle up on the couch in the living room and stay up all night long watching them run across the floor. We couldn't wait to go to school the next day just to catch up on our sleep. We would act like we had headaches, so we could get a pass to go to the nurse's office and sleep for two periods. We begged my mother to move out of that house. To make matters worse, Pete had moved in. His presence alone added to the misery in that damn mouse house. One night Keisha, Tee, and I were about to go out and get something to eat when we heard my mother and Pete upstairs arguing. We stopped at the bottom of the stairs to listen to what was going on. We listened to my mother yell, "Get the fuck out of my house…!" Then he shouted back, "I'm not going' nowhere…! "Tee started boiling, and before you know it, he was headed up the stairs. Keisha and I just started following behind him. Tee stood in the doorway to my mother's bedroom and said in the manliest voice he could muster up, "Pete, my mother wants you gone. Why don't you just go and leave us alone?" Pete jerked his attention away from my mother and shot a look of hate at my brother, roaring,

"SHUT THE FUCK UP AND STAY IN A CHILD'S PLACE."

My mother shouted at Pete, "Don't you talk to my son like that!"

"You need to teach them little bastards some respect," he spat out at her.

My mother yelled at us to go downstairs. But by that time, all respect had left the building because we were so ready to fuck this man up. We just couldn't deal with him anymore. Our hesitation caused my mother to yell at us again. "I said go downstairs!" Pulling ourselves together, we gave in and decided to listen to our mother's instructions. As soon as we got down to the bottom of the steps, we heard Pete's voice yell and call our mother a bitch. All the quietness jumped out of Keisha 'cause she turned around and screamed upstairs, "What you just call my mother?" He said, "A FUCKING BITCH!" Then he slapped the hell out of my mom. He slapped her so hard I swear I felt it. We all just looked at each other and said, "Oh hell no! He didn't just hit mommy like that." My brother put us in a huddle and gave my sister a stick that we kept by the door and me a telephone receiver. Then he grabbed a golf club for himself. He told me to go to the back steps and for Keisha to take the front steps while he ran upstairs. Tee ran into the room with the golf club gripped in his palm like a baseball bat and said,

"Why you just slap my mother, mother fucker?

" Pete hollered back, "Mother fucker if you don't get your little ass back downstairs I will slap you, then whoop your sisters' asses as well."

My brother just snapped and started swinging the golf club at Pete. The club clocked Pete right on the side of his arm. Keisha and I must have thought the same thing. Fuck the plan because we both ran up the stairs with our weapons, jumped in the fight, and started beating on Pete as well. We were hitting him all over his body. My mother was yelling for us to stop, but she didn't get in the way, so we continue to beat on Pete like the uninvited guest he was. He was bloody lying on our floor, and he wasn't moving at all. We thought we had killed him. We started getting scared because he really was not moving, and it did not look like he was breathing either. The funny thing is, Deep down, we really didn't care because he hit our mom. We dragged him out to the porch and even rolled him down the front steps. Then went back into the house and shut the door. We never saw that bastard again. We did hear through the grapevine that we banged him up pretty good.

That ass-whooping made our night that night. It even put a smile on my mother's face. She knew she had some crazy kids, but we shocked the hell out of her with that one.

She knew we were overprotective of her, but she was stunned after that. My mother moved on and found her a new boyfriend his name was Mark. He was all right. Mark was short, dark complexion, thinning hair not very much a looker; I didn't know much about him. After a few months of dating him, my mother decided we were finally going to move out of the "rat hole" and go shack up with Mark. So we were moving again, but this time it was not into our own house; we were moving into his home. I remember asking my mother, "Why, mommy? Why do we have to move in with Mark?"

# Chapter 7:

# CROWDED

"Everything has its wonders, even darkness and in silence. If you don't learn the easy way from those who care about you, you always learn the hard way from those who pretend to love you."

**AFTER WE SETTLED** into Mark's house, my gut proved to be correct. It was straight bullshit here. Keisha and I couldn't do anything. We had to share a full-sized bed in this small ass room; even in the projects, we had separate beds. Shit, we had separate beds in the "rat hole" we just left. Mark had so many rules, too; we had to come in the house no later than 8 PM when the street lights came on. That would not have been so bad, but the rest of his rules made even the smallest one make me want to choke him. We couldn't sit in his living room; we couldn't go in his refrigerator or turn on the TV without his permission. When we came home from school, we would have to sit on the porch for hours until he got off work to let us in. He said he didn't want anyone having a key to his condo. It was straight like living in jail in that man's house. I would complain all the time to Keisha that I couldn't take living here anymore. I would say, "He is not our father." None of that complaining mattered, though, because what was I going to do? I had Such a street mentality; it was killing me not to do something stupid damn near every night. My sister and I talked about asking our grandmother if we can stay with her, but we did not have the guts to ask her. Plus, she lived right across the street from Marina Village, so it would've been like we never left the projects. That was right up my alley. Although it would not have been a field trip living with my grandmother, I know she will never treat us that way. This man was getting on my last nerve, and I was becoming a ticking time bomb. Less than a year had passed, and my mother knew we didn't like living there. She finally revealed how Mark was behaving to us as if we were fucking prisoners. One day she finally decided to talk to him about how he was treating us. I felt good inside; I said, "Yea, mommy finally going to put Mark in his place." We really couldn't hear the conversation between them, but I guess Mark didn't like what my mother told him cause before you knew it, we were moving. I thought we were getting our place, but we ended up moving in with my Aunt Neet. She already had her brother, Tommy, living there with my sister Sharon and her daughter Nae-Nae, so we had to pack in on top of all of them right back in the projects. I always called Nae-Nae my Aunt because she was so much older than me.

I was happy to be back in the hood, but our living situation was the worst. I had to sleep in the bed with both Sharon and Nae-Nae. Nae-Nae and Sharon shared a room, so they had to push their twin beds together so that I could sleep in the middle. That was no fun sleeping between two grown-ass women, and the crack in the middle of the bed felt like I was going to fall right through in the middle of the night. Keisha slept in the bed with Aunt Neet, and Uncle Tom slept in the living room on the floor. My mother stayed somewhere else. I didn't know where my mother was staying. She used just to come by and give my Aunt money for us. Aunt Neet was an incredible person; we didn't get treated like Sharon, but it was nice of her to take us in. Summer is about to begin, and in the next few months, it will be time to go back to school. That means I have to create my hustle. Shit you know, 'stack enough money so me and my sister Keisha can have some nice clothes to wear back to school.' Hell, I was about to start high school. I had to be on point. Although Keisha had a job, it wasn't enough. She worked at a department store called Aims. Keisha was always thinking about me. Every time she would go to work, she would come home and tell me she picked out some outfits for me and put them on layaway. She would say to me how nice they were, what colors she picked out, and not worry about anything. I felt blessed to have a sister like her. She was always like a mom to me, no matter what the fuck I was doing. That's how close we were. Keisha would get our clothes off layaway and bring them home to me. I would be so appreciative of everything she bought. Sharon, on the other hand, had money of her own. She was getting designer clothes out of Macy's. As Keisha would pull our clothes out of the bag, Sharon would always tease us about how cheap they looked. We just ignored her because we knew how to put them together, so they don't look cheap. Deep down, she would piss me off, but I kept my cool. I love my sister and all, but she can be mean, too. She always said stupid shit to get under my skin. So that summer, Keisha worked, and I hustled in the PJs with my homeboys. I was selling drugs, lying, and using men for their money.

I made sure I did my part so that Keisha and I went back to school looking right because I was excited to go to high school.

# Chapter 8:

# TOMBOY

"Being who you are is just a chance to grow.
Life is very long progress; how you spend your days
is eventually how you will spend your life."

IT WAS MY first year in high school, and I was so excited. Keisha was already in high school, a grade above me, Sharon was in the 12th grade about to graduate, and Tee wasn't going to school at all. I would ask my sisters about what high school was like, and they would gas my head up with stories, saying, "It is nothing like elementary school." I could not wait to get to high school. On my first day, I was excited: no more 6th graders walking the halls. When I walked around, all I saw were my old classmates. The same people I've been going to school with since elementary. But when I turned the corner and walked to the other end of the hall, I was like, Hey! Now I see what my sister was saying. There were a lot of cute guys up in here. The only problem I had with that was that I hated dating guys in the same school. I preferred dating an older guy that I didn't have to see every day while I was in school; then. I could flirt with all my little friends and not have to worry about my boyfriend. A few months into high school, I started to grow out of that tomboy stage and started acting a little more feminine. I see those desirable girls getting a lot of attention and hated to feel left out, so I said it's time to boost my game up. I gave myself the ultimate make-over, retired the sneakers, and became more and more like a girlie girl. I got so popular. I had it going on in my school and my hood. Most of my friends back home in Marina Village were like, "Damn Gale, I didn't realize you were that cute. You look good all dressed up. "My friends would tease me and say, "You know you still a dude. You are just a guy in heels now." I would laugh, but I can't lie. They were right. I guess I can't get rid of that boyish mentality; it is too deep within me. It is who I am. Most people didn't know that I hated being real skinny.

It made me feel like I had no figure, but I had to get over that shit, so I kept my confidence up when I was around people. They couldn't know my weaknesses; they had to think that I thought I was perfect – but I didn't. I always kept quiet in school, though; I spoke when spoken to and didn't put my business in the streets. People that know me understood that quiet shit didn't mean anything. I was a no-nonsense person and accepted no bullshit from people, yet at the same time, I was fun to be around. I realize now what girls didn't really like about me; I was always around the fellas. Chicks were calling me a gold digger. I didn't understand why, though, because I was making more money hustling, running schemes, and stealing cars; I was making more money doing fraudulent activities than most of the guys around my way. They said I was arrogant and stuck up. I don't know why people used to get the wrong impression of me. Luckily I never really gave a Damn about what anybody had to say. I guess. They were just jealous because I was all about my paper, and nothing else never mattered to me. I had a theory about hanging out with a bunch of chicks anyway: It equals trouble, women love to hate and always have something to say about You.

This theory is not something I came up with off the top of my head; I have experienced female friendships in my life, and some of them have ended up crazy as hell. Most of them I'm still cool with; two became great friends and, one of my friends, I found out we were dating the same guy. When I confronted her about it, she didn't say yes, so I left it alone. But I knew there was more to it. I didn't care because, to me, he wasn't worth it anyway. I was enjoying the material things. People called him Bruno, but his real name was Tommy. He was from Bridgeport, 20 years old and handsome; although I was hitting my teens, I lied to him and told him I was 16 so he would date me. He was another guy with money, the type of guy that was balling, you know, the typical drug dealer from around the way who had nice cars, plenty of women, and a big spender. That man was giving me everything. He bought me my first designer handbag. It was a cute Fendi purse I wanted, so at no expense to him, I got it, and the material things started rolling in. Now I started coming to school looking fly; no more AIMS for me. My sister and I upgraded the inside of our tags. I dated Bruno for the first two years I was in high school. He wasn't shit, though. Outside of the shopping sprees, there was always some drama. I started to get tired of the lies and the women because I stayed arguing or fighting over him.

Everybody kept telling me I was stupid; he doesn't respect me, maybe because he was 20 and I was only 15. All these older women and younger girls started coming out of nowhere about their dealings with Bruno. Even my Friend came clean about how she had been messing with him as well. By that time, It was a rap for me, and I start feeling bad for her and try to convince her to leave him alone, but she was one of those gullible chicks who just wanted to be in love. She told me that she knew that he wasn't worth it, but she loved him anyway and could not leave him alone. I wasn't even mad when she told me all that; I damn sure didn't love him; I just loved his wallet after I stopped messing with him.

My Friend continued to deal with him. Suddenly I was on the other side of the fence; I started telling her to leave him alone. She was a cool chick, but she continued to stay with him and accept the bullshit. She was the type of girl who didn't care what anybody had to say – she had a lot to learn for herself, and she deserved better. Now me, I was on some other shit. After a while, I was like, "Fuck Bruno," I can get money from the next dude without falling in love; that was my M.O. I felt like if you weren't getting money, I was not messing with you. Everyone in Bridgeport knew that. A lot of Guys knew not to approach me if they didn't have a lot of money. The best thing for them to do was to stay the hell out of my face. Most men would say, "I wish I had enough money to date you. "I would smile and reply, "It is not all about the cash, knowing deep down I was lying my ass off because it had everything to do with the money at that time. But you can't let everyone know that you are only about them benjamins. Please, I would even take the average working man for everything he got. I know it wasn't right, but I didn't care. I was young, beautiful, and street smart, and that was dangerous. I didn't give two shits. All I cared about was money and what the next man could do for me. I had guys eating out the palm of my hands. It was not easy, but In a way, I wouldn't say I like using men, but I had to do what I had to do with the right person and to the right degree and at the right time. I had a purpose, in sort of a negative way - that is not within everybody's power and is not easy. Most of these men knew which one of them had a chance and which ones didn't, plus I had a short fuse when things didn't go my way. All that meant the most to me were money, respect, and family. If you didn't fall into any of those categories, then I didn't give a damn.

## Chapter 9:

# RIDE OR DIE

"Change and of course growth will take place when
a person has risked themselves and dares to become involved with experimenting with his or her own life."

**I HAD LEFT** my Aunt Neet's house and moved in with my Aunt Penny. She was another relative, my cousin, but since she was way older than me, I always called her my aunt as well. She was living on the west end of Bridgeport in a housing complex called The Evergreens. People called them projects, but they weren't. My Aunt Penny's ass was cool. She was more like my homegirl than my aunt. I spoiled her but, it was all good. I had no guidance. I started to do what the hell I wanted to do. I came in whenever I wanted to come in, went to school when I wanted to go to school, and I didn't have to hear anybody's mouth. I practically raised myself. As time passed, I started to say fuck my education. I just wasn't focused anymore. I skipped class half the time because I was too busy trying to hang out in the streets, doing what I did best - get money. One day I got up to go to school; I was hungover and tired from drinking all night and did not feel like going, but I dragged myself in and was miserable the whole day.

Shortly during 7th period, when it was almost time to go home, there were only 25 minutes left of class. I just got up, walked out, left the building, and never looked back. I just quit school, not thinking about my future at all. I just said, "Fuck it." At that point, I chose to give up and focus my attention on what I thought was necessary, and that was the streets. My boys around the way had put me on to some easy money that made sense to me at the time, but even poor decisions have their kind of purity. I started transporting drugs back and forth on the Metro-North train to Harlem, New York. At first, it was easy. I was getting three hundred dollars a trip carrying narcotics in a duffle bag, collect the cash, and bring it back to Bridgeport and vice versa. I went twice, maybe three times a week depending on how the business was going; I knew I was playing a dangerous game, and after a while, things did get complicated because Metro police were getting tips on people transporting drugs on and off the train. I began to get nervous, but I still took my chances and made my runs. I did it for about a year and a half before I got scared. My toughness was going out the window every time I saw a cop on the train or deck. Then they started having the police dogs walk the platform as well. That had me thinking, "Is this money worth it?" One afternoon when I went to Harlem, everything seemed all good getting on the train. On my way back to Ct. As my stop was slowly approaching, metro cops plus dogs were sniffing up and down the platform. I got so damn nervous; I didn't want to get off the train. All I could think about was getting caught. I figured that the freaking cops would bust my ass if they pass by me. For all, I know it's me they are seeking. I had drugs and money in my duffle bag, hoping there was no way those dogs wouldn't be able to sniff me out. Because we would put coffee grounds on top of the drugs to mask the smell, but I still felt like those dogs would smell me if they got close enough. So I decided to stay on the train until I got to the Milford stop, coming up next.

The conductor came up to me and tapped me on my shoulder. I almost jumped out of my skin. He said, "Ms., you missed your stop." I played it off like I was sleeping. I had a cup of coffee in my hand to throw off the smell of the coffee beans all in my bag. I started to ask him stupid questions to throw him off like, "How far is Milford from Bridgeport,' because I need my mother to pick me up," knowing damn well I knew where I was, and finally, my stop was here. I was scared to exit, but when I got off the train. I just started walking until I saw a payphone. I didn't want to use the ones on the platform. My peoples kept paging me because I passed my stop, and they were waiting for me in Bridgeport. I walked as far away from the train station as I could. Finally, a few blocks away, I called my peoples to pick me up and let them know I was straight. The conversation was short; they came and got me in less than 30 minutes, and I went back home. Man, I never felt so damn relieved in my life. That tough shit went entirely out the window. All I was thinking to myself was, "Damn, I'm just a teenager. What the fuck am I doing? I better stop this shit; hell, I get more money from a man I'm dealing with than I do transport drugs. So I decided to say fuck it.

It's time to retire. I'd rather put up with a man's shit than go to jail for a long time. This shit had me thinking. I need to prioritize my life and stop making the streets my top priority. I think there are aspects of it that definitely illuminate my bad decisions if I don't stop now these decisions will start to negatively affect me, "but that's what I was thinking. I guess you can say I had the mind of a 27-year-old woman; I was very mature for my age. My game was tough, and I was only getting better at my craft. I was popular in and out of town. I knew how to carry myself in any situation, whether it was that hood mentality or business level. I could transform into a "high class chick" in a minute, and for some reason, they always thought I was someone important, and that's the role I played without actually having to tell them what I did for a living. Fantasy was a necessary ingredient in the way I rolled; it was a way of life looking through the wrong end of a telescope. Which is what enabled me to look at life's complex realities? The truth is they didn't care. My flashy clothes, jewelry, and expensive purses were full of money; I had them thinking big, and that's how I wanted to keep it, but more and more, it seemed like many individuals didn't like me. I guess it was because of the way I carried myself. "I don't know; I never considered myself an average girl. When others went left, I went right; when they think low, I thought high, and I wouldn't have it any other way. I remember the day before I quit school group of girls rolled up on me, jumped out of a car, and started beating me. They all had weapons: One girl had a hammer, the others had a stick. I couldn't believe I was getting jumped, and I didn't know what to do but fight back. I was scared, yes, because I didn't know what was happening. All I knew was I had to fight back. I was only wondering which girl was going down with me. Somehow I got my little ass out of that situation and ran to school with my face covered in blood. I went straight to the nurse's office. I wasn't hurt bad, though; I just had a gash in my head from the hammer and some deep scratches on my face. I know if I were to jump some chick, her ass would still have been lying on the ground; that's how I knew my revenge was going to be sweet. The school called my mom, and she got there in about 25 minutes. My mother came in, asking a million questions. She wanted to know who they were. The school wanted to call the cops. I just kept saying I was OK because I knew I would get my revenge when I caught their asses. I was pissed off – not because I got jumped but because they messed up my face, and I was not having that. The word spread quickly. Before long, everyone was talking about what happened.

All I needed was for Augie to find out what happened. Augie was the boy my parents raised since he was little. His folks were friends with my parents, and they would leave him with us all the time. Augie never wanted to go home with his original parents; he loved staying with us for some reason. We just looked at him as part of the Family, so I called him my brother. It was my brother. He was Puerto Rican, a little shorter than six feet, but he acted like the biggest man in the world, and he was wild as shit, the definition of crazy. He didn't care about anything or no one at all. He was the gangster-type who didn't give a fuck. He didn't even give me time to get home, and he was already at my house. Augie yelled out the window at me, "Get your ass in the car…" "Hold up, wait a minute, we will catch them chicks one day," I said, frustrated.

"I already found them…get in the car," he demanded. So I got in the car without any argument. We drove over to the east side of Stratford Avenue, a terrible area where everybody hung out, but Augie knew where they were. Before he could even put the car in park, Augie jumped out and started punching them girls, one by one, in the face. I grabbed a bat from the car, started swinging it from side to side, hitting anything and anybody that was in the way. I don't usually condone a man hitting a woman, but the girls deserved that shit, especially since they messed with me.

My family didn't play that. My brothers and sisters had my back. They were always there without any questions. We ride or die for one another. When my sisters found out, they were pissed off because they didn't get a piece of the action. I eventually realized that those chicks jumped me over some guy I wasn't even seeing. They just assumed it because he and I were close. After a while, nobody would mess with me because of my brother. That boy played no games. It got to the point where Augie was so out of control I didn't want to go anywhere with him. One day my homegirl Mel, Augie, and I were chilling' in the projects, and Augie was begging me to take a ride with him across town. I told him hell no, I wasn't riding anywhere with him. He had gained too many enemies; word on the street was that some guys wanted him dead, but that didn't mean shit to him. My brother always had at least two guns; on his hip.

We knew that damn-near the whole city hated his ass and for anybody to be in the car with him was risky, and I wasn't in the mood to take that risk.

"I love you, but I'm not getting in the car with you."

"What the fuck; you scared? I got this; nobody going to do shit to me."

"OK, I pass."

"Fuck you then," he laughed out. Then he turned to my girl Mel and asked her.

"Yo, Mel! You gonna take this ride with me?"

"OK, Augie"

"That's what's up."

"Where are we going?" We'll be back quickly.

I have to pick something up, and Gale's punk ass doesn't want to ride with me. Mel was like one of the fellas; she had that hustler's mentality like me. She was my partner in crime. About an hour went by, and Augie and Mel still have not returned. I was mad as hell; all I could think was their asses done went somewhere without me and left me here. Twenty minutes later, I got a phone call saying Mel and Augie got shot up on the Avenue. I started screaming into the receiver at the person on the other line. I don't even remember who it was because after the news, so much was a blur. Everything seemed to go in slow motion. Playing back the story now still feels like hearing a broken record. They were riding on the Avenue they stopped at a light another car pulled beside them, pulled out guns shot up your brother's car I didn't want to believe it was true. I rushed to the hospital and discovered that my brother had got shot in the stomach, along with Mel. I could not believe it, I could have been in that car. They could have died. Thank God they were going to survive.

What if I would have been in the car? With my luck, I would have been the one that didn't survive. I was in a daze for the rest of the night. I could not sleep thinking of Augie and Mel in the hospital. The fact that I could have been there with them or no longer here. I couldn't shake the feeling. Maybe it was time for me to make a change in my life. The next day I went to visit Augie at the hospital. He looked over at me as I entered the room and said, "Come over here sis, and give me a hug." I walked over to his bedside and hugged him tightly. He looked at me with those deep eyes and said, "I don't know if I could have lived with myself if something happened to you.

I just kept thinking, damn, my little sister could have been in the car." Augie softly wept out. I just put my arms around him and said, "It's OK, Augie. As long as you and Mel are OK, that is all that matters. All you need to think about is getting better." He smiled, "That's why I love you so much."

When Augie and Mel got released from the hospital, Mel immediately began to change her ways. She calmed down a lot; I guess you could say that this was her wake-up call because she was not hanging out like before. Augie, on the other hand, did the complete opposite. It was like the shooting made him worse. He became a wild, raging animal, loose in the streets. We thought he didn't give a shit before; well, he didn't give a fuck now. That boy started robbing anyone, walking around, and shooting at random people. Everyone was afraid of him. Every time he would go outside, I would get so nervous, especially when he went to house parties or nightclubs. He had so many enemies that any party he went to, he was bound to walk into someone that doesn't like him. But you couldn't say anything to him. Augie loved the clubs. My sister Keisha would always say that something awful is going to happen to Augie if he didn't slow down. The whole family was worried about his life. We knew he is going down a road with limited destinations. My sister Sharon had a baby with one of Augie's friends, whose name was Stephon. At first, Augie was not feeling his boy messing around with his sister; mainly because Stephon was a gangster-type guy like Augie, and he didn't want him to treat her like he did all his other chicks. But after she had a baby with him, Augie just accepted it. Sharon moved out of Aunt Nita's house into another apartment in Marina Village, where she started to raise her daughter on her own because Stephon was locked up in prison. She moved right across from the building where we grew up. I used to go to her place a lot, to spend time with her and the baby. One summer morning, I walked into the kitchen and saw Augie acting real strange.

He took his necklace from around his neck and put it on my

beautiful two-year-old niece, then kissed her on her forehead and told her how much he loved her. I looked at him and said, "What's wrong with you? Why you look so down?" "No reason. I'll be back in a little while." "OK." My sister came down and saw Augie leave out the front door. I looked over to her with an expression like, Damn, he is acting weird this morning. Not even five minutes later, we heard loud gunshots coming from outside. Sharon ran down the apartment stairwell, and I followed. As soon as she opened the front door, one of my homeboys from around the way yelled, "YOUR BROTHER JUST GO SHOT IN THE ALLEY RIGHT ACROSS THE STREET." Sharon ran across the street and found him lying on the ground in a puddle of blood, a gunshot wound on the right side of his temple. Sharon fell to her knees down beside him and started screaming at the top of her lungs, "Augie, please don't die, hold on Augie, you're going to be all right…" But Augie was not all right; the shot was fatal, and he was dead. I just stood there, frozen. I could not move; I didn't want to move. I didn't want to see him like that. It was just too much for me, so I just stood there and watched as Augie lay dead in my sister's frantic, shaking arms. I didn't even move as the ambulance pulled up, put him on the stretcher. My sister sat there, hypnotized with horror, soaked in Augie's blood, screaming, "Why did they do this to my brother?" I grabbed her up. "Come on Sharon, we have to be strong." I pushed out as much of my cracking voice as I could manage. I helped Sharon to my car, and we followed behind the ambulance to do whatever paperwork was necessary. I called my mother on the way down to the hospital to let her know what happened. She was hysterical, but she had to pull herself together to notify Augie's biological parents of his death. My mother's next call was to Augie's girlfriend, Shalonda, who was five months pregnant at the time. There was a large gathering at the funeral, and Augie's friends were so loyal to him they paid for the funeral as their way of paying their respects to him. He lay there looking so peaceful like he was in a deep sleep, well-deserved sleep, but the left side of his head was very swollen from the gunshot wound; I leaned over and whispered to him, "Now you don't have to worry. God always forgives. You are in a better place now." Then I kissed him before they closed the casket and smiled as tears ran down my face. As days will pass and turn into years, I will never forget him. He taught me to be strong, but sorry, I'm letting him down because I can never accept that he is no longer here.

# CHAPTER 10:

# JUDGMENT DAY

"Sometimes, the slightest shifts in the way we look
at things, a seemingly insignificant change in perspective can and will alter your life forever."

**I HAD BEEN** in this damn place for two weeks and I just didn't know
how much longer I could take it. I lay on my bare green, thin, vinyl
mattress, looking up at the ceiling and wondering how the hell I was
going to get Dr. James to give me a good enough recommendation to
get out of this damn place. I had opened up to him and told him the
story of my life. Shit, I was opening up to him about things I didn't
even remember I had gone through. The truth is I was feeling better. I
never really talked to anyone about any of the stuff that had happened
in my life and it kind of felt good to have someone there to listen to
me with no interruptions. Since I am one of four children, I always had
to fight for my affections. No one was interested in hearing me go on
and on about my problems, because most of the time they had their
problems to deal with. Dr. James listened though he didn't even really
give advice. He just sat there and listened. James wasn't stupid; he only
wanted me to tell him about how I got in there. He wanted to know
what drove me to...to swallow prescription pills and chase it with a

razor blade across my wrists. He wanted me to talk about my daughter. Just the thought of it sent chills up my spine. I was hoping if I gave him enough about all the bullshit I had been through growing up, he would feel sorry enough and let me go home, but I guessed wrong. He wanted to know about Shanice…my attempted suicide. I just didn't know if I was ready to talk about it yet. I wasn't sure if I was really strong enough to go through the hellish details of the past seven years of hell that led me there.

Dr. James had a smug smile on his face as I walked into the room. It was as if he could smell the fear in me. I was petrified to go to his office that day.

He and I both knew that I was ready to get out of there. And he knew that I knew what that was going to take. He watched me as I slowly walked over to the hard metal school chair I had grown accustomed to. His eyes squinted as he noticed my hands shaking – my nerves were going a hundred miles a minute. I sat in the chair and looked him dead in the eyes.

"How are you feeling today, Ms. Johnson? You look a little nervous," he said smugly.

"I guess it's just your office. I always get nervous when I come in here."

"Why, this is a safe place."

"Yeah, just like Confessional at the Church."

"Well, I don't know if we can go that far, but your secrets are safe with me." He smiled.

"Where did we leave off?" I asked.

"Augie had just died…" he said with interest like he had been waiting to hear what was next.

I sat back in the metal chair and took a deep breath. I knew this was about to be a long session. I just gave into defeat and started to spill.

"After Augie's funeral, I decided to move back to my mother's house…»

My mother had just found a new place on Johnson Street the house was directly in front of Marina Village, right among all my aunts and grandmother. It was a one-bedroom apartment, but I didn't care if I slept on the floor. I was tired of running the streets. I was getting out of control, living with my Aunt Penny. I just couldn't take it anymore – there was something that changed in me because I was feeling drained. My aunt kept a house full of company; there were always a bunch of people in and out all the time. Half of them were drug dealers using my aunt's house to cook and bag their drugs. The other half of them were guys only looking to hang out. Don't get me wrong, her house was the party spot. We had a lot of fun there, but it was starting to be too much for me. Plus, I was still really young. I think I just tried to grow up too fast.

When I called my mother and asked her if I could move back in with her, she shot me down real fast. "Hell no, if your ass wanted to be grown enough to walk out of here and live with Penny, then you need to be grown enough to take care of your damn self. All you ever did was disrespect me, doing what you want when you want.

Now you're crying, wanting to come back home."

I was so mad when she finished shouting at me, so I slammed the phone down and hung up on her. I was pissed off. I wanted to punch her in her face, but I would never in my life hit my mother. Keisha had been staying with my grandmother. She wasn't happy about it, but she liked the fact that she was stable. After a few weeks, my mom finally gave in and said it was OK for me to move in with her. I was so happy. I moved out of my aunt's house immediately; no one even knew I was gone. My mom and I slept in her bed together. She wouldn't let me sleep on the couch because she didn't want me wearing her sofa out. And she did not play when it came to her stuff; she did not like anyone messing up her things.

Man, it felt so good to wake up in a quiet, clean, peaceful house – I loved it. It was nice and calm for about the first week at my mother's house. It did not take long for me to find my way back into partying and bullshitting again, though. But this time, it was nothing like before. I had calmed down a lot. I just wanted to live a peaceful life without all the drama.

Unfortunately, bullshit finds me like a magnet; soon I started getting into new shit. I was fighting damn near every other day behind someone else's mess. There was always drama with some females about men they thought I messed with. I couldn't be outside for more than an hour before some chick found something to say to me or one of my homegirls. My sisters and I were never scared when it came to fighting. My problem was that I didn't like to fight, so if you push me up against a wall I am going to attack you.

My mother was going crazy with me staying with her. She couldn't take my wild ways anymore. So she begged me to slow down, saying, "One day you are not going to make it back through these doors if you don't slow down. It does not make any sense. You are too pretty for that. You need to start acting like a young lady before you end up like your brother." She had me thinking when she compared me to Augie. I felt I owed her to change. I hadn't changed completely because I was still partying and hanging out late but I wasn't as wild as I used to be. My mother's words stuck in my head all the time. It was hard for me to walk away from my life in the streets.

I was like a hood celebrity. I was enjoying the attention I was getting; "They say if you hunger for the attention, it is an enemy for self-love. I didn't want to be looked at and grab attention, I would rather be seen more for my intelligence, and not being just another girl seeking attention.

So on one particular night, I went to this club called the El Canyon, across the street from the projects. I only went to certain clubs because I was underaged, though I never acted my age so it was hard for them to predict. They assumed I was young because of my looks. The owners never gave a damn; they knew me very well because I used to sell them cocaine. I always looked out for a few club owners and bouncers.

It was cool because it worked out when I needed favors. That club was the shit; everything went on at that spot, from shootouts to fights every weekend. That didn't stop my ass from being a regular there, though. I was right in the mix of everything that went on. They knew me and I knew them. Soon I would get to know someone else who loved El'Canyon as much as me, because that is the night that I met my kid's father – the man who put me through seven years of straight hell.

# Chapter 11:

# MR. M

"The worst thing in the world is holding onto someone
who doesn't want to be held."

HIS NAME WAS Martinez; he was about 6'2", 210lbs; real slim. He kept his
black hair in a low wavy Caesar haircut. Everyone knew him around the
hood because he was another street hustler affiliated with that gang life.
He wasn't the best-looking guy I ever saw, but he kept himself up and
had lots of money, so that made him very attractive to me, as usual– and
to every other chick. I first met Martinez at El' Canyon. He was there
with all of his friends and family, celebrating his release from prison.

He had just come home after a four-year bid. My friends and I were
sitting at the bar, taking our last sip from our second round of drinks,
when I saw him looking at me from across the room. I played it cool and
pretended like I didn't notice him. I'm the type of girl who likes for a guy
to approach me. Martinez watched me the whole night. I just ignored
him; it was too easy because I wasn't really into Spanish guys. It was just
his street status that had me wide open.

Before I could signal the bartender to bring my girls and me another
drink, a guy placed a glass down in front of me. I looked at him with a
semi-confused look and asked, "Where did this come from?" I already

knew the answer to my question.

"Martinez., the guy over there having the party," he said, pointing over Martinez's direction. I already knew all about Martinez from these women on the streets that's been waiting on his release. Now on his first-night home look, who ends up in the bar with him. Sorry ladies: yawl can cancel your plans cause Gale about to lock his ass down.

I accepted the drink, looked over at Martinez, and raised the glass in the air to let him know I was thankful for his gesture. I half expected him to walk over and try to holler at me right then, but he didn't; he just continued to party with his family and sent me and my girls' drinks all night.

Right around the time, the club was about to close. I told my girls I was tired and wanted to go home. The truth is that I was drunk; I knew if I stayed here any longer, my little ass would pass out who knows where, and I wasn't in the mood for that shit tonight. I never knew how to say "when" until it was too late, which always ended in regret the following day. As soon as we reached the bar's exit, Martinez swept in out of nowhere and blocked me from leaving. "You were just going to leave without saying goodbye?" he asked, almost demanding an answer.

And I was a little turned on by his forwardness; I smiled and answered flirtatiously, "I saw you were with your peoples, so I didn't want to bother you."

"I've been waiting for you to bother me all night."

"Really?"

"Yeah, I thought you were going to come over after I sent you the first drink. Then after the 3rd drink and you still didn't come over to holler at me, I knew I was going to have to work for you."

"Well, that's true. You will have to put in some work if you're interested in me."

"I am willing; your little sexy ass can have anything you want from me."

"Be careful what you say, 'because I demand everything."

I was just used to paper chasing, and Martinez had just gotten out of jail from serving a four-year bid. So, I knew he would do whatever I said just for a taste of me, and I was ready to make him work for it. Martinez called me the next day. When the phone rang, I had a feeling it was him. I did not want to answer because I wanted to see if he would call back or not. But then I remembered that his ass just got out of jail and probably have a list of women whom he would rather see. So, I decided to pick up the phone before he got to the following number. You know, the second chick always be the thirstiest, sitting by the phone waiting for a guy to call. A chick like me doesn't be thinking about his ass half the time. He is lucky if he catches up with me. When I answered, Martinez immediately took charge of the conversation. I was impressed.

"Hello?"

"What you are doing?"

"I was just getting ready to start my day. What are you doing"?

"I'm outside. I came to take you to breakfast."

"What?"

"How long you about to take?"

"You outside?" I whispered out as I slowly started towards the window.

"Yo, listen. Get dressed, and I'm going to wait here until you ready. Then we can go eat wherever you want." Oh boy, I hate unexpected shit, but I thought that it was cute of him. I didn't know Spanish guys had it in them (smiling), but Martinez acted like a black guy. Even the way he spoke, there was no Puerto Rican thing about him except for his skin color. It took me about thirty minutes to get ready. Mind you; he called me while I was still in bed. When I got outside, he didn't even complain about how long I took. He just asked me if I was ready.

"Yes, Martinez, I'm ready."

"You sure? We might not be back for a while."

"What's a while?"

"Do you have a curfew?"

"No... I just didn't know breakfast was going to be all day (laughing)."

"Oh; ok. You got jokes this morning. I like that (smiling)."

I just sat in the car, and we headed off to Frankie's Diner on the other side of town. I didn't want to go. There was always someone there that you knew to pop up. I was the type that didn't like people in my business. Plus, I was sneaky at the time. As we walked into the diner, I ask Martinez if he didn't mind sitting in the back. He didn't ask questions, although he did give me the strangest look. Martinez and I had a good breakfast; we stayed at breakfast for about two hours, not eating much. It was our conversation that increases our stay. After we had finished, we just drove around the city for a while, sightseeing in every hood. I didn't know the reason for that, but I had nothing to do anyway. After riding for hours, Martinez asked me if I wanted to go to the mall. Hell, I'm not turning anything down that might benefit me, so I said yes, and then asked him, "Why are you taking me shopping?"

"I wouldn't ask if I wasn't interested in you."

"Ok, baller; off to the mall we go."

Martinez looked at me and said, "I like you." You are so beautiful."

I wondered why he wanted to spend money so fast, but I wasn't going to ask him. As we entered the mall, I went straight to Macy's shoe department and found the cutest pair of red heels. Martinez bought those, then picked up another pair and said, "I think you'll look really nice in these." As he paid for them, I couldn't help but look at him and say to myself, "Shit. This is only our first date, and I like the guy already. "He wasted no time in spoiling me. We went into four more stores; I bought a few outfits, then we went home. Even though we didn't do much, it seemed like my whole day had gone by so fast. As he was dropping me off, everyone stared at us as he walked me to my door with all the bags. I saw the hate on everybody's face like I was a bitch. I loved every minute of that shit. I thrived off the haters; they help me keep my shit together.

"Shit," I thought. "He might be the one…" I guess Martinez was the one because there was no way I was going to give another girl a chance for Martinez to mess around with.

# Chapter 12:

# SURPRISE

"What do you do when the only one who can stop
your tears is the only person who made you cry?".

**OUR FIRST FEW** months of dating were cool. Martinez would take me shopping every Friday throughout the year. It was no limit to what I can have. Money was not an issue, and price did not matter. I would grab whatever I wanted. He would even let my sister Keisha come with us to pick out a couple of outfits for herself. He knew how close she and I were, so he made sure she got everything I got.

Martinez would give me absolutely anything, but honestly, I deserved it. I always had my shit together. Men have dug how I carried myself because I have always kept myself together from head to toe. But to the women out there, I wasn't shit but a gold digger.

I was good to Martinez and faithful, something I had thrown out the window a long time before because most men out here will take you, for granted and you have to act just like them, or you will get swallowed up in the madness. I learned fast, so when necessary, I could be a straight bitch with a lot of balls. Martinez and I had been dating for six months. It was the best six months between us. I never thought that I would find such a person in my life. I never felt so. Every time

I would call him, he answered. When I needed something, he got it. If anyone in my family or just anyone I knew needed something, he would take care of it. He slowly made me fall for him.

Martinez took me to Atlantic City on our six-month anniversary and handed me a velvet box with a diamond tennis bracelet and two plane tickets to Puerto Rico. He wanted me to go with him to visit his grandmother and his mom, who had recently moved down there.

She had wanted to move back there to be close to her mother. I was apprehensive about meeting another side of his family, although I had already met his immediate family, like his sisters, children, brother, and mother. I didn't know how they would react to me. I was more concerned that I wouldn't be good enough for him. I was more nervous about what his grandmother would say about our age difference because technically, I'm going to be nothing but a child in their eyes. So, I decided not to tell them my age; Hell, Martinez doesn't know my actual age, so I think this is not a big issue. People are already talking about our relationship on the streets. It's just pure jealousy. Martinez captured all my time, and even though I was no longer hanging out as much, I just stayed to myself but kept my ears to the streets. My girls would report to me every day about people talking silly shit about me. They asked, "Why this grown-ass man taking care of this young girl like that?" Martinez didn't seem to pay it any attention, and neither did I. Fuck it; I was happy, and that was all that mattered, and we were not letting gossip ruin our inner peace; that was a critical necessity to us to have peace in our heart and minds.

Getting off the plane in Puerto Rico was like stepping into the page of a magazine ad for an exotic vacation. Martinez had it all set up. A driver was waiting for us at the airport. He drove us to this beautiful hotel in San Juan as he waited for Martinez and me to change our clothes into something more comfortable to suit the weather. I felt we were a bit overdressed to go to his grandmother's house, who lived more towards the country on the city's outskirts.

His grandmother's house was nothing I expected, but she seemed very content with her living arrangements. All of Martinez's family were there to greet us: his mother, stepdad, and some of his cousins. They gave us big warm hugs. Everyone was so lovely to me; they treated me like I was a part of the family.

Every day we did something new. We went jet skiing, sailing, sightseeing, and lots of shopping. Martinez had us acting like tourists. We ate at the most beautiful restaurants in San Juan, drank at damn near every bar, and partied the whole time that we were there. It was like a dream; this was the first time I have been anywhere like that. I'd never been anywhere but to New York City, South Carolina, and Philadelphia. Every day I would be so tired from running around I would pass out as soon as we got back to the hotel. After the first six days, I was ready to go home. It was nothing like where I was from, and damn near, no one spoke English.

Most of the time, I felt out of place, especially when I was around the Martinez family. We had done everything that was there to do in Puerto Rico, some stuff twice. And for some reason, I was starting to feel sick. I wasn't sure if it was something I ate or the amount of drinking I was doing, but I wasn't feeling good, and I just wanted to go home.

I started to get agitated with the heat, as well; the day before, the temperature got to 99 degrees, and that felt like the coolest day since we been here, and going out to his grandmother's house every day didn't make things any better. Her little window didn't help against the heat.

Martinez's mother stayed in another part of town; her home was in the process of renovation, so going there wasn't an option, and by the seventh day, I was over it. Martinez wanted me to go water skiing with him, and there was just absolutely no way. He begged me so much, I almost considered. But I had been feeling dizzy from the heat, and I didn't want to torture myself anymore by going out in direct contact with it. I told him that he could go with his cousins without me. I wanted him to still get the most out of the trip, even though I wasn't feeling well. I just wanted to stay in the room for the day and relax. I woke up the following day, throwing up everywhere. I thought I had food poisoning. Martinez was there; as I lay on the bed, Martinez's mother even noticed that I wasn't looking too well. She couldn't speak English well, so she looked at Martinez and spoke to him in Spanish. He looked at me with a kind of funny shock on his face. Before Martinez could open his mouth to translate, Martinez's mother put her hand on my stomach and said,

"You pregnant, mommy."

I could have fainted just by the thought. Martinez laughed and then looked at me as if he were trying to figure out if it was true.

"She's not pregnant," Martinez said with a half-laugh, half question.

"I know a pregnant woman when I see one. And this girl is pregnant," she said to Martinez so sternly, like she was there in the room holding the light while the sperm broke through my egg.

"You're pregnant?" Martinez shot a look at me like I had set him up.

"No. I'm not pregnant. I think I have food poisoning."

Martinez's grandmother was standing in the other room, listening to the conversation.

"She said in Spanish, why you don't just go to the doctor's when you go home to be sure?" she chimed in. The look on Martinez's face lit up like a light bulb had just turned on in his head. "We're not ready to be parents all of a sudden, it felt like a dark cloud had settled on top of my head, and rain just started to pour right in the middle of my romantic paradise; this was not on the agenda. Had I known it was a possibility I was pregnant, I would have gone rock climbing.

My nerves were through the roof by the time Martinez got back. I could not sit down. I just kept pacing back and forth around the room, waiting for him to walk through the door. I was not sure

how he was feeling about the whole thing either. The look on his face when his mother brought the entire pregnancy thing up was almost horrified. And he ran out of here so quickly I wasn't sure what was going through his head.

As soon as he walked through the door, he asked all of us if we were ready to go to the festival. I asked him where he went, and he replied, "I needed some air." My heart started beating fast as we all walked out the door. I could feel the pounding in my chest with just the thought. I just wanted to say, "Leave me the hell alone." Martinez was lucky I was in his territory because of the way I was feeling. I could have cussed everybody out in that damn room, starting with his mother for even putting me through this shit. Even if she thought I was pregnant, she didn't have to announce it to the whole family. I could have dealt with these illusions alone with my own family; here, I was in another state without access to any of my relatives or friends. If we were ever in doubt about what to do, which I was, it was a good rule to ask myself what I should've done. I never let my sense of morals prevent me from doing what's right, especially if I were pregnant. I'm just a baby myself; that was what scared me the most, despite me already being an out-of-control teen. We judge ourselves by what we feel capable of doing, but others back home were going to judge me by what I had already done. After all this worry, I decided to go out and get a pregnancy test. I took the test out of the box and squatted over the toilet, trying to position myself for the perfect angle to get my pee on it without squirting all over me. When I finished, I held the stick in front of my face and watched the little dispenser as it changed from a white color to dark pink. Then I saw lines begin to appear. Then there it was—a big, fat plus sign. I was pregnant.

"Damn, I mumbled, scared. I guess it's time to tell Martinez that his mother was right. Sometimes I feel like the elderly have a gift of knowing shit, but she had me thinking. Martinez's family, especially His mother, was into that whole lighting candle in her home for blessings, putting garlic at her door to keep evil out, rosary beads around a big Buddha statue. Stuff like that. Martinez once told me, "She wasn't into evil voodoo, but hell, voodoo is voodoo to me no matter which way you practice it."

# Chapter 13:

# FANTASY

"All fantasy should have a solid base in reality, but we all
live in a world of fiction to keep our reality away from us."

WE DECIDED TO leave four days earlier than our original flight. Once I
broke the news to Martinez, I needed to get back home to my family.
At least I knew there was an explanation of my madness and why I felt
sick in Puerto Rico. But I don't know how to feel about this whole being a "mom" thing. Surprisingly Martinez was excited about me being
pregnant. By his original action, I thought he was going to be upset.

I tried to share his enthusiasm, but I didn't quite know how I felt
about it yet. I was scared and in no way excited. I was afraid because I
didn't know how to be a mom or raise a baby. But on the flip side, deep
down, I guess I was happy about one thing, though, change. I'd needed
to change a lot of the things in my life. It was time, my lifestyle and
all the partying, fighting, and bullshitting – and being a mother was
the perfect excuse to stop being a "bad girl." On the returned flight,
Martinez asked me if I wanted to move in with him. I agreed; I figured
that would ease the blow when I told my mom. I wasn't too nervous
about speaking with her, though, because I had already put her through
so much. I had been doing what I wanted for so long. What could she

say now? Martinez's family didn't care; it was just another child added to his list. My child would make Martinez's third; he already had two beautiful children by two other women: a little boy and a little girl. All I could do was hope for a precious little girl for myself and calmer life. Responsibility is like a string: We can only see the middle of it, but both ends are out of sight. The willingness to accept responsibility for one's own life is the source from which self-respect springs onto me now.

After all, the messing up, I started to tell myself all the disrespect I dealt my mother; although I'm still young, I'll be growing up faster than I expected. I did all that shit to feel "grown-up;" I just never understood why I thought I needed to grow up so fast. I finally had an answer: I experienced that life through a constrained lens of immaturity and perceived adulthood as a condition of greater freedom and opportunity.

But what is there today, in America, that very poor adolescents like myself want to do but cannot? Not much: We decide to "do" drugs, "have" sex, "make" babies, and "get" money (from our parents, from the State, through crime, or—like most women like myself—off men).

When I got to the house, I did start to feel more nervous about telling my mom. As soon as I began to part my lips, she shut me down. Her ass said, "I already know you're expecting, so what are you planning to do? You have no job or education."

I just started laughing.

"I don't find anything funny."

"How the heck did you know I was pregnant?"

"A mother knows."

Then we both just laughed. I told my mother that I was moving out and Martinez and I were going to get our place. She was more concerned about me, though, and what I wanted.

"Are you sure this is what you want to do?" she asked in her motherly way.

"Yeah, Ma. We can't live here in your one-bedroom apartment with you."

"You right, and you weren't going to live in here with me either because I'm done raising babies."

For the first time in a long time, my mother and I just sat there talking and not arguing. I don't know if I was already maturing or what, but I just wanted to be with my mother when I found out I was pregnant. We got close that night. She started telling me all about her experiences with men and how they treated you when you lived with them. She said, "When you move in with a man, running them streets all times a night will not be accepted, and it is not lady-like, especially if he's the one paying the bills. Add in the fact that you're having a baby, you're going to have to grow up, and all your childish ways will have to come to an end.

"I know, and I do feel like I am ready for this," I confessed to her. "OK."

Then she looked at me hard and walked out of the room. I sat there for a while, thinking about our conversation; trust me; I was listening. I knew my mother had been through a lot with different men. I saw everything she went through, especially with my father, and I would be stupid not to trust what she said. But I was ready, and I knew Martinez; he was not like the men she had. He was sweet and caring. He also loved kids, so I knew he was going to be a good father. Just the way he reacted showed me that he was a good man. I didn't even have to suggest getting a place to live; he just knew what the next thing to do was. Martinez is a real man, not a drunk like my father. I knew Martinez would take care of our child and me, and that is all I needed. I was a young girl in love, so it made sense that the next thing to do was start a family. It was what I needed to slow my behind down. I was excited about my future. I was happy about the baby, about my relationship. Life could not have been better at that moment. It was like Martinez was my knight in shining armor, come to rescue me from my past life, and I had been waiting to be saved for so long, and this was what every little girl dreams of, and I got it.

# Chapter 14:

# REALITY

"The unreal is way more powerful than the real because nothing
is as perfect as you can imagine it."

OUR FIRST PLACE was beautiful. It is only a one-bedroom apartment;
it's not super fabulous, but it's good for our first place. It has a well-
sized living room with windows from the floor to the ceiling when you
enter through the door. What I liked most about that apartment is the
view. It is the main focal point for this place. For me, something about
the windows makes an apartment look good. To the left is a small dining area with enough space to put a round dining set and an extended
kitchen with lovely cabinets and floors. The bedroom has a nice size
walk-in closet, and I was happy about that because all I do is shop, and
a girl like me has to have somewhere to store her belongings. Martinez
gave me a stack of money and told me to purchase anything I wanted
to furnish the place as long as I was comfortable. He said his child's
mother deserved only the best; boy, did I start smiling from ear to ear
when he said that.

I ended up spending over ten thousand dollars on furniture. I
bought everything brand new, all the way down to the silverware, but
in reality, I had to because we didn't have anything. I thought I was

living in a dream; now I could finally enjoy being pregnant. I had nothing but positive thoughts about having a live-in boyfriend. For the first time, I felt as though I were in love instead of just being with a man to survive. I felt like someone cared about me.

I remember my grandmother telling me if you don't like how things are in your life, change it! If you're headed in the wrong direction, God allows U-turns! And I felt like he was pointing me in the right direction now because I've done and seen everything and overlooked a great deal. Now I want to correct it little by little.

I decided to go back to school to prove to my mother that I was growing up, and especially to myself, that I could do the right thing. So, Martinez paid for me to go to school to become a CNA. When I graduated and got my first job, I felt a new independence level that I had never felt before. I truly felt like an adult. I began to listen to my mother by not running the streets anymore. Instead, I spent my time working, cooking, and cleaning. My mother always taught us to take care of the home first, drilling in our heads that laziness will only cause you pain. I was feeling like a real housewife, and I loved it. I wasn't about to miss an opportunity to make my man happy, even if I had to leave him alone to do it. That's how much I loved my relationship and how special he was making me feel. I was not struggling to survive; I didn't feel stupid and dependent on anybody. I was happy in love and free of all the bullshit that had always found me. It was almost too good to be true.

I was on my job for two months, working the third shift from 11 PM to 7 AM. It worked well for Martinez and me because he was always in the streets hustling half the night, so by the time I got home, he would just be coming in. It felt like we worked the same schedule, except my job was legit. I loved my job and, most of all, my independence. The only thing was I was five months pregnant, and no matter how much I appreciated my job, I didn't feel like being there or anywhere but home in my bed—being pregnant sucks.

I had been feeling sick one night. I kept throwing up and having these dizzy spells. At one point, I almost fell straight on my face, but one of the nurses saw me and caught me before I dropped. My supervisor sent me home early to get some rest. She had children, too, so she knew what I was going through. I didn't call Martinez to tell him I was coming home; I figured he wasn't there anyways because he was usually in the streets, and 2 AM was prime time for him. I was surprised to see his car when I pulled into the parking lot, but I was happy he was home so he could comfort me and take care of me like he always did.

As I walked up the steps to my apartment, I could hear loud music playing in the building. I figured it was coming from another apartment, but I noticed it came from my place as I got closer to my door. I just thought Martinez must have fallen asleep listening to the music and didn't realize how loud it was this late at night. I put the key in the door, and as I opened it, I could not believe what was in front of my eyes. Martinez had another woman in our home. We just moved into this place – we hadn't even broken it in yet, and this bastard will disrespect our house like this. I wanted to kill him. I stood there in complete shock as he is utterly wrong. I think there has to be a reason for this: but of course; he denies any wrongdoing and turns things around on me; We always kept a bat by the door, so I grabbed it, then I went to swing, but he held the bat from me as soon as I drew back at him. Instead of trying to defend himself or explain why he had this woman in my house, this man had the nerve to call me out my name and "shouted you supposed to be at work."

A feeling of hate shot through my body as tears started falling from my eyes. I screamed back at Martinez, "I got off early…I wasn't feeling well because of OUR baby."

He had the nerve to say,

"You supposed to call me if your ass was leaving work." "Why the hell do I have to call you to come home to my house from work?" I yelled, choking my words out at him.

Martinez snatched me by my arm and said, "I do what the hell I want to do and bring whoever I want in my house; you pay no bills here." Martinez finally let go of my arm and escorted the girl out the door. I was devastated! I couldn't believe it. I was pregnant with our child, and he was able to treat me like this. I was so hurt. I was too embarrassed to go to my mom's house or anywhere else. I could not deal with having to answer any questions or telling anyone about what had just happened. I was already humiliated enough. I sat there like a fucking dummy, asking myself why Martinez acted like this everything was so perfect. "Why?

How could he do this to me?!" It took everything out of me not to find a knife and slice both of their fucking throats.

I gave Martinez the evilest look I could muster up. As they say, if looks could kill, his ass would have dropped dead right in that living room.

I felt so uncomfortable being in that house. I didn't want to sit or lie down anywhere in that apartment. I had so much anger inside me I didn't know what to do with myself. I felt like my whole world had turned upside down, and there was nothing to catch me. I just wanted to die, but I tried not to be angry. I knew I couldn't make others act the way I wished them to. I ran into the bathroom crying, slammed the door, and started screaming at the top of my lungs, "God, why is this happening to me? I thought he loved me!" I just kept yelling out to God, "Why?" I had never felt any pain like this before. I kept having to take deep breaths because it felt like my chest was going to cave in. I didn't want to have a baby anymore, especially by a man who could treat me like this. I started punching myself in the stomach and screaming out, "I HATE HIM, I HATE HIM!"

When I finally came out of the bathroom, Martinez was gone. He had just left me there and didn't say anything. Martinez didn't give a fuck about what happened or how I felt and left our home for two days. He didn't call, check on me, or anything. When Martinez finally decided to come back home three days later and didn't say a word to me, like nothing ever happened. He didn't even try to apologize; he just walked into the house, went into the bedroom, and shut the door.

I just sat there shaking my head, thinking this man has got to be kidding me! Is this how our relationship was going to be full of complete disrespect and abuse? People used to say he was verbally and physically abusive; now I'm starting to believe those rumors. I began to think that Martinez treated me like a princess as a cover-up to who he was: "AN EVIL BASTARD." Is this what I have to look forward to Name-calling?, Being pushed around? Trying to take in the fact that I was about to become a prisoner in my own home, I couldn't move. I just sat there looking at the room's door, frozen. About an hour later, Martinez came out and walked over to me sitting in the same chair in our dining area as I was sitting in when he came in. He wrapped his arms around me, and I could feel a cold chill go through my body.

"I'm sorry," he said playfully.

I thought to myself, is this man for real? But I didn't say anything; I just sat there not knowing what to say. I was feeling such a significant number of various feelings on the double. I wanted to execute him, yet I was reluctant to be without him since he was my child's father.

I didn't hug him back. I didn't move at all. I couldn't say anything because I could already see that a conversation with him would have gone nowhere fast. I was mentally exhausted, and I didn't have it in me to argue.

I just wanted to put all the fucking drama behind me and move forward because I knew I was stuck there with him deep down in my heart. And as long as I was pregnant, there wasn't going to be much I could do about it. I just had to anchor myself fast in my faith.

# Chapter 15:

# PRISON

"We have to learn to be our best friend because sometimes we fall into the hands of our worst enemies."

**THAT NIGHT MARTINEZ** had another woman at our home marked the first of many horrific nights to come. Martinez started to get controlling, abusive and became a serial cheater. He would be with different women all the time and even stay out for days if he felt like it since he was paying all the bills, buying the food, the clothes, and providing me with transportation; that was his house. I was his property. I guess this made Martinez feel entitled to give orders, control, and abuse. It was so shocking to me that he could be this way because of how he was at the beginning of our relationship. It seemed like after I got pregnant, all hell just broke loose. But "My Heart Was Taken by Martinez., Broken by Martinez., And Now Is In Pieces Because of Martinez." It's hard to tell my mind to stop loving him when my heart still does. Sometimes it's hard to love someone because you're so afraid of losing them......"
UGHHHH"

When I was coming close to the end of my pregnancy – around eight months in – and found out we were having a little girl. I felt it was an ideal opportunity to get to a more prominent place because I wanted to set up a baby's nursery. The apartment we were leasing was on a month-to-month basis, so we basically could move out at any time. I thought he would agree with me, but instead, Martinez asked why I'm not too fond of the place we are residing at already. I told him that it was not the fact of me liking the home or not; it was just that I wanted a room for the baby since she would arrive in about a month. Martinez's son was always at the house with us as well. He was almost a year old and stayed with us more than he stayed with his mother. It felt like I was practically raising him. He was the cutest little thing, and I fell in love with him instantly. Since we were all there together, I just wanted the kids to have their separate rooms. So, Martinez gave me the OK to start searching elsewhere. I wanted everything to be perfect since I felt like things in my relationship were doomed; this was my first child, and I didn't want her to lack anything.

I was also getting more and more excited about the baby as I came further in my pregnancy. So, I called the realtor and began our search for a new rental home. It took us three weeks to find a suitable apartment. It was a three-family house in the city's west end of Bridgeport. We took the apartment on the main floor; it has three bedrooms, a lovely eat-in kitchen, a front room, and a large yard. That was a plus for me because of the children. Martinez didn't help much with the move; it was mainly my sister Sharon and I who was also pregnant; we moved everything by ourselves with some other family members' help. I was so pissed with Martinez by the end of our two-day moving experience. He decided to call and ask if we needed any help. I just hung the phone up on him because that was a dumb question to me.

Why would he even ask that when he knew we needed help? At this point, I could not take any more stress; I just wanted to wrap things up and get everything over to the new place. I said to myself; we shouldn't have put all this strain during our pregnancy as I was hit in the stomach a few times by the furniture during all this heavy lifting. I started to feel a sharp pain in my stomach, and it kept getting tighter and tighter. The pain was indescribable. I had never felt anything like it in my life before and couldn't wait until this move was over.

It was about the end of the day, still no Martinez. It was like he didn't even give a damn. I could have had a miscarriage for all he cared. My sister Sharon on the other hand was pissed off. She was cussing Martinez out. She said to me, "You know you can always find a new baby daddy." Sharon never gave a damn what came out of her mouth. She was going to say whatever the hell she felt like, no matter what. She didn't care. Martinez didn't come back until late that evening. I pretended to be asleep, but the truth was I couldn't sleep; he had me so angry, with many thoughts running through my head. I never thought my pregnancy would be like this. My fairytale had a horrible ending. I thought that we would have been happy and in love.

But I just felt like I was a prisoner trapped in a cell with this man, who had suddenly decided to treat me like I was nothing. Yes, he provided well, but that was where it ended. He just wanted to make sure he looked good in the streets, our house was lovely and that I looked nice, but behind closed doors, he was a monster. I was the prisoner, and he was the watchdog.

# Chapter 16:

# SHANICE

"I have come to realized that Earth has no sorrow for me
that Heaven cannot heal."

**A MONTH LATER,** Sharon gave birth to her fourth child, a little boy named Carl. I still had 3 ½ weeks left until my due date, and boy, I could not wait. I felt like I had been pregnant forever, maybe because of all the aggravation in my relationship. I couldn't wait to hold her; at least she would keep a smile on my face in the house of hell with Martinez since he was crazy and never let me do shit. I had to ask permission to go out to my mother's house. I couldn't even hang out with my friends anymore. Deep down inside, I was thinking, "Just because I'm miserable, I shouldn't let him stop me from enjoying life."

I felt like I was his slave. I had to make breakfast, lunch, and dinner for him every day; it didn't matter if I was sick or tired. I even had to ask permission to go places. He didn't care. I used to believe that holding on and hanging in there were signs of great strength. However, there were times when it took much more strength to know when to let go, move on, and not look back because his physical and mental abuse was destroying me. I was not used to something like this; I used to be tough! I used to be a bad girl. But it seemed like all that had disappeared, and I was allowing someone to take control of my life. Hell, my mother didn't even have control over me like this, so why was I allowing it?

One morning I had an appointment with the doctor but woke up late, so I couldn't make Martinez breakfast. So, I just got dressed and left, thinking nothing of it. Martinez never came with me to the doctor unless it was to drop me off at their office door. When I came home that afternoon, as soon as I walked back into the house, that bastard started yelling in my face. I screamed out, "What the fuck you are yelling for?" He said, "for not making my breakfast." I looked at him with all the hate in the world in my eyes. "You got to be kidding me, right? "He didn't care that his argument made no sense. "You know I had to go to work, and I need my fucking breakfast." Martinez had just become so evil and foul those last five months; it was puzzling because, for the first six, he had been the exact opposite. I just looked at this mother fucker like he was crazy; he couldn't just grab something to eat. And what was that about going to "work?" That man had just gotten the first real job of his life, at a U-Haul place up the street from our house. He must have felt so goddamn important now. He only got the job because the cops were all over his ass, wondering how he made all the money we had. The job was bullshit, but it made him feel like he was a real man now; he started acting like he was a businessman or some big corporate hotshot or something. I felt like I was going through endless hell with this asshole. And it would just keep going, on and on.

Later on, that night, around 1:30 AM, I went into labor. I had gotten up to go to the bathroom when a big gush just poured out of me. Shit is this really about to happen.

I was so glad I was about to have this baby. I was more than ready. A part of me still couldn't believe it; with all the stress I had gone through over the last months of my pregnancy, I thought for sure that I would have a miscarriage. By the grace of God, I had survived through the whole nine months.

I was only in labor for about two hours. I was scared as hell, but I can say that I was more nervous than scared. I didn't know what to expect because of the crazy baby stories I heard from everyone. It seemed like as soon as I went into the delivery room, I just pushed her out. She didn't give me any problems at all. Martinez almost passed out; his punk ass couldn't take all the blood, screaming, and chaos that was going on. You would think a person like that can act all hard in the streets can take a woman giving birth. But I guess, as they say, men are the weaker species.; it was so crazy for him to see me push a baby out, but he pulled through it in the end. I was so excited when the doctors put her in my arms. I couldn't stop looking at her. I kept saying, "She's so beautiful… but why is she so white?" I was smiling from ear to ear, but she didn't look like me at all; she looked just like Martinez. I didn't care who she looked like; she was still precious. "Wow," I realized at that moment that I was indeed a mommy now. I wanted to name her Ashley Shanice, but Martinez preferred Shanice Ashley. Either way was pretty to me, so I let him win, and Shanice Ashley it was. Martinez kissed me on my forehead and said, "Good job, Mom." I looked at him and said, "That's the nicest thing you've said to me in months. I can get used to this." He smiled and said, "Let's call her Shy-Shy for short." I told him that was perfect for her.

For the first time, I felt like I had accomplished something. After my delivery, I felt like a woman, and it felt great. Martinez already had a daughter, so that made two beautiful daughters and a handsome son for him.

For a moment, I was sinking in all the joys of motherhood and how Martinez was treating me. But I wondered how long this was going to last with me. Plus, I wished that he would appreciate me a little more. Martinez was the type where it was either his way or the highway. He knew he had complete control over things and especially over me. That was the part I couldn't stand. He was the breadwinner, yes, I understood that, but I guess that made him feel like he had the upper hand over me. Yes, I had what every girl wanted as far as some nice cars, jewelry, pocketbooks, shoes, stacks of cash, and a beautiful home, but that was all material because there was nothing pleasant about what was going on inside my house, nor inside of me. I know God wouldn't have put me in situations that I couldn't handle, but I asked not for a lighter burden but for broader shoulders. One happy moment of love, or the joy of breathing in the fresh air on a bright, summer morning, is not worth all the suffering and abuse Martinez dealt me.

# Chapter 17:

# LIGHT

"Lately, life has been screaming too much out at me.
Maybe it's not meant to be, but I beg to be helped out
this mess because I had become a stranger to myself."

THE TRUTH IS I was very unhappy in our relationship. I was always miserable. I wished to be more independent. I hated that Martinez felt like he could control me. It was killing me on the inside, and it was starting to show to my family. They knew what was going on—I couldn't hide all the bruises. Pretty soon, the whole city of Bridgeport knew what was going on. Everyone knew that this fabulous life that I was trying to portray was not so great on the inside. After a while, my personal life was the talk of the town. Everywhere I went, people were whispering about how Martinez would beat my ass and how he had complete control over my life. Then all the cheating that he was doing out in the open was just straight disrespectful. People were saying how stupid I was for allowing him to do what he did to me. What's crazy is that I never cared about what people said about me.

Shit, people talked about me all my life. But this time, it was different because what they were saying was accurate, and the truth does hurt—I was stupid. I tried to drag my ears away from trouble and avoid it all, but everywhere I went, someone always had something to say. Martinez's cheating had pushed me to the point where I used to follow him around in different cars. Once I borrowed my cousin's new Nissan because he wasn't familiar with it and saw him with all types of women being disrespectful towards me. It was like he didn't even care how I felt, almost like I didn't even exist. I was so hurt every time I would confront him about the females. Martinez would lie right to my face.

When I confronted him with the truth that I had been following him around, he threatened to leave me. The craziest thing about that was I would beg him to stay. Inside I felt like I could not breathe without him. When he would start to walk out the door with his bags, I would grab him by the ankles and beg him not to leave me. A few times when I did that, he would kick me anywhere his foot landed and pull me off him, yelling, "Get the fuck off of me." One time he spits on me, but that wouldn't be the first time he did that.

I didn't care what he did or said because I was so in love. I would tell him, "Go ahead and stomp my brains out. I would rather die than let you go." Thinking back, I should have never begged him to stay. That just gave him the upper hand to treat me more and more like shit. I was acting like a deranged woman, making a complete fool out of myself. Although I hated how he treated me, I still had to be with him. I could not stomach the thought of him being with another woman. I don't know what it was, but I had to be with him no matter what. I was just plain stupid to put up with his crap. I deserved so much better.

But with all the drama that was going on in my life, I still managed to keep my job somehow; I was able to balance working full time, taking care of two kids, and waiting on Martinez's hand and foot. I was trying to make the best of our relationship, and I knew that I had to keep him happy to do that. All the energy I was putting into Martinez and our household was draining me. No one was giving anything back to me; I just felt so lost and prayed for brighter days. A storm had started brewing over my head that I had no idea how to fight. Life as I knew it was turning upside down – and there was nothing I could do to stop it.

# Chapter 18:

# NIGHTMARES

"My ears were steadily betraying me, so I curled myself
around a bunch of lies."

SHANICE HAD STARTED to get sick. We moved out of our three-bedroom
and into a two-bedroom condominium. It seemed like a decent place
at first. Then we found out it was the condo from hell—the home was
infested with roaches. There were so many damn roaches. I used to
wake up with them crawling all over us. I was afraid to fall asleep at
night because I was scared they would get on my baby. So I stayed up
to keep them off of her. No matter what I did, I had to watch Shanice
closely; otherwise, the roaches would be crawling all over her. For example, if I went to take a shower, I would come back, and there would
be three or more roaches crawling on her body. I would grab her and
brush them off of her. I have seen roaches before, but I had never seen
them like this in my life. Those roaches took over our condo.

Before bedtime, I would stuff our ears with cotton so they would
not crawl inside of them. I had to buy a net to put over Shanice's crib.
I would have it tucked in so tight under her just in case I dozed off to
sleep; they wouldn't be able to crawl on her.

The roaches had taken over every inch of the condo. It got to the point where I just stopped going to the grocery store because they would always get in our food. I couldn't take living there anymore. I tried everything in the world to get rid of those critters, but nothing worked. Not even 4 ½ months into our lease, we got the hell up out of there. I found a two-bedroom townhouse nearby and made sure this time that it was not infested. We were moving so much I was becoming disgusted by it. If it wasn't an infestation, it was Martinez feeling paranoid about the cops.

Our moving around was bringing back memories of when I was young and living with my mother, how she would always have us moving around because of her boyfriends or us getting evicted from one place to another. I just wanted to be settled and create some stability for my child that I never had. I didn't want her raised like me from house to house. I wanted our family to be together in one place that we could call home. As soon as we moved into our townhome, that was when my life as a mother became more complicated than I would have ever expected.

One afternoon around two o'clock, I laid Shanice down in her playpen for a nap. She was ten month's old now and so full of energy. Putting her down for nap time had become the few hours I could truly rest. So I went to the couch to lay down, instantly falling asleep. When I woke up, I realized four hours had gone by, and Shanice was still asleep. When I went in to check on her, her lips were purple, and her face was discolored, and she was not responsive.

I started screaming for Martinez to come downstairs. I was crying, telling him something not right with Shanice. He grabbed her, and we rushed her to the hospital and arrived in minutes. When we got to the emergency room, the doctors wasted no time running her back to a room. They started putting all these tubes in my baby; they even hooked her up to a respirator because she struggled to breathe independently. We were frantic. I had never been more afraid of anything in my life. Just the thought of my baby dying had me in panic mode. Even Martinez was nervous; he kept pacing back and forth around the hospital room.

Shanice stayed in the hospital for six days, and after all the tests and uncertainty, she was diagnosed with asthma. I could not understand how she just developed asthma. When she was born, she was in perfect health. It was not until we moved into that infested condo that she started to get sick. People were telling me that roaches could cause you to get asthma. I never used to pay it any attention because I thought it was just something someone heard and had no hard facts. It sounded stupid at first. I thought Shanice had inherited it from the family; both of her grandmothers had it. But the thought lingered in my mind. I never looked any further into it because I got so busy just taking care of Shanice. I was just worried about keeping her better. I started taking her to a private doctor.

I felt more comfortable dealing with a specialist who would know her condition instead of always bringing her to a clinic. Her new doctor was Dr. S. She was awesome! She just put Shanice on a few inhalers to control her breathing if she had an attack. After a while, her condition started to worsen, so Dr. S ordered a nebulizer machine for us to have at the house. Dr. S also made us come in three times a week just for precaution. But throughout the weeks they administered medication, it didn't seem like anything was working. Her health only got worse. There were times when I had to bring Shanice into the emergency room two or three times a week. My mind started to suffer, and I often broke down in tears. Doubt is a pain too lonely to remember that he has a twin brother named faith.

Between Martinez and Shanice being ill, I was going crazy. I was so stressed out. The verbal and physical abuse, the lack of control, the unknown; everything had gotten so bad, and our problems began spilling out in public. Martinez would fight me anywhere, at any time he got angry at me. Half of the time, I didn't know why he was upset. One night I went to a nightclub with my sister Sharon to get out of the house. I hadn't been out in a while. My sister Keisha kept an eye on our children for us. I just wanted to go out and have a little fun. I just needed a break for the night. I knew Shanice was in good hands because I never left her with anybody but my sisters, Martinez sisters, or her grandmothers. They were the only ones that knew Shanice's condition inside and out. They also knew what to do if she had an attack.

Before we left for the club, I decided to call Martinez so that he would know where I was, and I wouldn't have to hear any shit. As I went to pick up the phone, both my sisters yelled out, "Fuck Martinez." So, I decided to hang up the phone; shit, they were right. I was sick of consulting with him over every move I made. Plus, I figured it would be really quick; we were only going to get one drink and then go back home. Boy, was I wrong? When we got to the club, I immediately hit the bar to settle in. I got a drink and started talking to my girlfriend, who I used to hang out with before I got locked down. Not even 45 minutes later, I happened to turn around and look towards the door. Three guesses of who walked in? You got it: the man from hell.

I wasn't even surprised when he walked in because that man always tracked me down. For some reason, he knew where I was. When I saw Martinez, I already knew what time it was just by the look on his face. I just continued to sip on my drink and talk to my girlfriend. We were laughing and joking about old times. Sharon had gone onto the dance floor. Before I knew it, Martinez grabbed me by the back of my head and slammed my face right into the bar. Everyone just looked at him in shock. I heard someone say, "Martinez, what the hell did you do that for? Chill out, man; it's not that serious. Your girl was just chilling." That just pissed Martinez off even more. He hated for someone to interfere with our relationship. Martinez started blacking out on everyone. He started yelling, "This is between my wife and me." He was always calling me his wife even though we never got married. When I was pregnant with Shanice, he had proposed to me, and I said yes, but I would never marry a man like that in the back of my mind. I ran out of the club, bleeding from my forehead. I was extremely embarrassed. I got into Martinez's car because I knew he would not let me leave with anyone else. Sharon ran out after me, begging for me to get out of his car, but I couldn't move. I just sat there crying and telling her that I would be alright. Courage is something I didn't have. I was full of fear; I was a coward, and I wasn't brave enough to fight back.

Sharon started calling me a stupid bitch; making fun of me, trying to get me to fight her. In a way, she was right. "I am a stupid woman. "That's just how I felt. It was just not right for him to carry on like that. Martinez kept screaming at her to mind her own business. They started going at it. Sharon was screaming, "That's my sister. Who the hell you think you are to tell her where she can and can't go?" Martinez got so mad; he pushed her. Sharon pushed him back and sprayed him with pepper spray. That spray didn't do anything but turn him into a monster. Martinez wiped his face with his shirt and charged directly at Sharon. Thank God someone from the club grabbed him and told him to chill because he was out of control. Once people got him a little calm after that embarrassing scene, he slammed the car door shut and sped off. We stopped by Sharon's house to pick up Shanice. Keisha got up in fright, wondering what was wrong and why I was crying, then spotted the cut on my forehead and got upset. I tried to calm her down, telling her I was fine, but she didn't want to hear that shit either.

She knew Martinez had something to do with it, but she knew there was nothing she could do or say to me to make me leave him. Falling in love with him was simple but falling out of love is simply awful. I believe that everything happens for a reason. People change so that you can learn to let go. Things go wrong so that you appreciate them when they're right. You believe lies, so you eventually learn to trust no one but yourself, and sometimes good things fall apart so better things can fall together. "I don't know; They say love is full of pains and sacrifices, but it also takes two for love to work. I felt like Martinez didn't care about anything but himself, and I hate the fact that I was allowing myself to suffer and hurt so much? Martinez cursed me out the whole way home. He told me I was no good and better straighten out my ways before regretting it. He said, "No man wants a woman shaking her ass in the club." But I was sitting at the bar. This fucking guy. Sometimes we women are afraid to let go because we lack self-confidence, and the worst thing to do is to walk away from an unsuccessful relationship and put it behind you. It is not a matter of chance, and it is a matter of choice; it is not a thing that we ask for; it is a thing to be respected.

According to Martinez, I was every awful name in the book by the time we hit our street. When we got in the house, I started grabbing my things to leave. I was so afraid of that man. He was screaming, "We'll get the fuck out of my house then. Once you start carrying yourself like a lady, then you can come back home. I couldn't believe what I was hearing. I looked at Martinez and asked, "Are you for real? Was I dreaming?

I asked him, "Why the fuck is you like this? It's 1 AM in the morning." He said, "You can go back to your sister's house for all I care." I was pissed off. I told Martinez, "You should have just left us there." He said, "You can go to hell for all I care." I felt I was already there. I was looking for my one-way ticket of courage to get up out of Dodge. When I went to grab my car keys, he snatched them out of my hands. Martinez always took my car away from me when he got mad because he had bought it; I guess that was his excuse to take them any time he wanted. It was just another way for him to control me. I felt like jumping off a cliff, building some wings on my way down to fly away from his ass because I had enough of his shit.

*Chapter 19:*

# BREATHE

"Every breath is a choice. In reality, you live until you die. The problem is that many of us in this world today can't handle reality."

AS YEARS PASSED by, I was dealt with the same shit every day. Things were still the same with Martinez, Shanice was getting bigger, and she had been spending her little years in and out of the hospital, almost dying twice. Her lungs had collapsed several times, and her condition was degenerative. She was turning three in August, and it was a blessing because of how severe her asthma was. We spoiled the mess out of her, and everyone adored her. She was such a strong little girl. She constantly had to take Prednisone, a steroid for her lungs, plus all of her other asthma medications. She needed to get on her breathing machine every two hours along with a dose of steroids, doctors' orders!

There were also a lot of stipulations that we had to follow to keep her well. We couldn't have carpet or stuffed animals, and She could not be around smoke or in cold or hot weather for too long. She couldn't even play with the kids for more than 20 minutes at a time or be in a swimming pool for too long because those things would trigger her asthma and cause her to have an attack that could either put her in the hospital for weeks or result in death if not treated fast enough. I couldn't even imagine it taking her life. Whenever my daughter would have an asthma attack, I could fit my whole fist in her chest cavity. That was how deep her chest would cave in. She would struggle so badly to breathe. I never saw a child or adult struggle so hard to catch their breath the way she did.

I used to cry so much because I didn't know what was going on. I kept stressing to the doctors to take more tests because the medications weren't working. In my heart, I felt like something else was wrong besides asthma.

The doctors would tell me that they could not do specific tests because she was too young. I had never heard of such a thing in my life. I use to bring my daughter to the emergency room so often, one of the doctors by the name of Dr. Zen had the nerve to say that it was something I was doing that was causing Shanice to have severe attacks. He insisted that it was me and not the medications or treatments that they were giving her. He was accusing me of neglect. You can call me many things, but never say I would do anything to harm my child. Dr. Zen had convinced himself that it was me hurting my child, so he called DCF (Child Protective Services) on me.

When they walked into my daughter's hospital room and introduced themselves, I was in shock. I couldn't believe that Dr. Zen had called them. The social worker told me that Dr. Zen was concerned that I was not doing everything to care for my daughter's health, which was why she was constantly in the hospital. I thought it was a joke. I just sat there looking at the social worker. I had no words. I was just so in shock at what the lady was saying to me. I couldn't believe it. I knew it wasn't the social workers' fault; she was doing her job, but I was upset at her and everyone involved in the situation. My family was in the room with me, and they were more shocked than I was to hear this. They were always there by my side every time my daughter went into the hospital. We would take turns rotating shifts so that I could get some rest or go to work.

Martinez never stayed at the hospital with us. He used to come up there for 30 minutes and then go back into the streets. I used to look at him and say, "Don't you want to spend time with your daughter here in the hospital? You act like you don't even care."

His favorite excuse was, "I have to work." That was nothing but bullshit to me. Martinez had quit the U-Haul job a long time ago, so all he did was hustle all day and fuck around; instead of being there, I would get so damned mad at him, knowing his child needed him around.

Shanice started doing ads for United Way; she became their little spokesperson for children with asthma. She was showing them how to use their inhalers and machines. She was so smart - my little princess. United Way used to throw these dinner parties, honoring people who were a part of their organization. At one of the parties, they honored Shanice. She had done a commercial for the program and a pamphlet ad. The people there just loved her; they were so amazed at how a three-year-old could accomplish so much and help other children who were battling the same illness. Shanice was so amazing to me. Just watching her handle herself like a little lady even though she was sick, you would never know. She took it like a trooper. But I knew the exact thing she was going through. I knew how she couldn't sleep; her throat would close up, waking her up in the middle of the night. That was tearing me up inside. I felt so helpless. There were so many times I would ask God to let me trade places with her. I didn't want her to suffer anymore. I would have done anything to have been able to take her pain away.

*Chapter 20:*

# INTRUDERS

"In this cruel world today, we barely have time to react,
let alone rehearse."

As THE YEAR went by, Shanice's condition continued to worsen, and DCF would not leave me alone. They were sending social workers to my house once a week to check on the environment. They would check to see if my house was clean if I had food in my refrigerator, proper medications, and anything else that would indicate neglect. They were wasting their time with me because I kept my house immaculate. Even before I had Shanice, my home stayed clean. I am just the type of person who can't stand a dirty place, and I'm OCD at its finest. When the social workers would come by, they would be so impressed at how tidy and organized I was. They would go into the refrigerator and see that I had everything in its place. Shanice even had her little section so she could reach all of her juices and snacks. I hated keeping leftover food, so everything was always fresh. All Shanice's medications I had stored in a proper place where she could not get to them and organized according to the time she needed them. Everything was so together; my home was a shining example of everything but Child Neglect.

Finally, after two months of the investigation, DCF decided to drop my case. The social workers kept giving me rave reviews about how neat and well kept my house was, how smart and beautiful Shanice is. DCF had to contact Dr. Zen and let him know they found no signs of neglect. I wish I could have seen Dr. Zen's face when he heard that. Though, Shanice's condition still was not getting any better. We continued to come in and out of the hospital weekly. I asked Dr. Zen repeatedly to run more tests on her because I felt like something else had to be wrong with her. But he would not administer further tests because he said she was too little – I thought that was bullshit. I wanted to find out what the hell was making my baby go through all the pain she had to suffer. The more he refused further testing, the more miserable he made my life. And to make matters worse, he continued to call DCF on me, even after the case was closed. Martinez was still up to his same shit. He bought things that I needed but didn't help me much with our daughter at all. Martinez was not there bringing Shanice back and forth to the hospital; he was not there most nights when she had to hook herself up to the breathing machine. The only thing he was there for was financial support, which made him feel like he was doing something. I was going through a lot with Shanice being in and out of the hospital and Dr. Zen bringing DCF back into my life. My life was in an uproar, and now my period just stopped coming. I had my mother bring me to the doctor to check out what was wrong with me. Honestly, I thought that it was stress making my hormones act up. Come to find out; I was pregnant. I could not understand how I had none of the symptoms:

My stomach wasn't showing. My period was still coming on. There were no signs at all. I was just pregnant. And there was nothing I could do about it. I didn't want to have any more kids with Martinez. I was so mad at myself because I knew it was my fault. I had not been on top of taking my birth control because of everything I was going through with Shanice, so it was my carelessness that got me back in this situation. I was mentally exhausted. I felt like I was trying so hard to hold onto my sanity, but it was slowly slipping from my grasp. I couldn't even mask my pain anymore. I knew I needed to be strong for my child and my family, but I was breaking down, falling apart. Every day I felt sick to wake up. I was so depressed and holding all this anger and frustration inside of me. I felt like I was getting nourished by depression. I wasn't eating, barely sleeping, and the worst part was I had to remember to pull myself together and be healthy for a whole new child. This motherhood thing is a tremendous job, and it got to the point where I had to schedule my nervous breakdowns. The anxiety attacks became a part of my daily routine. But they kept me alive because at least I knew I was still breathing and not living in a nightmare. Outside of the anxiety, I was mostly just numb. I had shut myself out so far from my family because I was embarrassed by all the shit I was going through with Martinez, but they knew what it was. And thank God for them because when it was finally my time to break, I knew where I had to go; like they say: Home is where the heart is.

# Chapter 21:

# ENOUGH

"I wish I had all the answers to everything, but in reality,
I'm just tired of asking all the questions."

MY SON ANTHONY was born with my mother and sister Sharon in the room. Martinez came right after I pushed Anthony out. My mother was the first one to notice that Anthony wasn't crying. The doctors rushed him down to intensive care for tests, sticking tubes in him and placing him in an incubator. Later they came up to my room and informed me that he had aspirated in my fluids as I was pushing him out. I was released four days later, but I might as well have just stayed because Shanice had a severe asthma attack, so we had to rush her to the emergency room. Thank God she was not admitted because I would have had two kids in the hospital at once; because Anthony was still in intensive care.

I had to go up to the hospital every day to visit my sick son, and Martinez had decided to take a trip to Florida. He claimed he had to go because it was a trip he had already planned with his friends. In my mind, I knew that was a lie. I knew he was probably going with some woman, but at that point, I didn't even care. While he was on his little rendezvous, I was coming home from the hospital at night and packing my shit up. I had a trick for his ass. I was going to be out with both my kids when he came back. It was not like I needed him there anyway. He was never there for the kids or me. He was driving me crazy and adding more stress to my life with all his lies, abuse, and bullshit. His trip was convenient for me because I was able to openly get rid of my furniture by selling it to my friends. I needed the extra cash, and since I was moving in with my mother, all I needed were my clothes and the babies' things because she had everything else.

Martinez told me he would be gone for a week, so I tried to get everything done before he got back. The only thing that was slowing up my move was that Anthony was still in the hospital. I would not leave my baby up there without me all day, so I would spend my days with him instead of moving my stuff. Two days before they released Anthony from the hospital, Martinez came back home from his trip. I was holding Anthony when he walked into the room. I could tell by the look in his eye he had already been by the house. The first thing that came out of his mouth was, "What's going on?"

I just looked at him blankly and muttered out a slow, quizzical, "What?"

He raised his voice a little. "What's up with all the packing?"

I gave in and just let it all out. I told Martinez, "There is no need for us to even have this conversation. I can't do this anymore. Our daughter is sick, our newborn son is in the hospital, and you want to take a vacation."

I told him our relationship was not working for me anymore. I was just miserable and tired of all the nonsense.

He looked at me with a funny expression and asked, "Where are you going to go?"

I told him I was going to stay with my mother. Then I slid in slickly, "What do you care? You are always kicking us out anyway."

He stood there acting like he cared and held Anthony's hand, looking all pitiful. I just left him there, carrying Anthony in my arms as

I went down to the cafeteria. And by the time I got back upstairs, Martinez was gone. I couldn't believe it. Apart of me wanted to chase him down in the parking lot and scream at him to find out where he was going. What was so important that he had to leave his family and sick children? I was so fed up with him at that point that I knew I was making the right decision – I had to leave. If I ever had any doubt, it had gone out the window. Martinez had done enough to me. There was nothing else left for him to do but kill me – and I was not going to let that man kill me. So one of us had to go, and it may as well have been me because I was the one who had to carry around this heavy load. So I had to be the one to finally just let it go and move on with my life while I was still young and had the opportunity to change it.

When I got home that night, Martinez was not there. He came in not too long after, wanting to talk. I let him talk while I barely listened. I was past any talking point. It is what it is, and I was out. I was so tired; I drifted off on him. I asked Martinez if he didn't mind if we could please continue our conversation in the morning. He was OK with that; he probably thought he had me. But the following day, I made sure I got up early. I was out of the house by 6:30 AM to see my son. I knew I had to see him very early because I had to take Shanice to the doctor in the afternoon. My mother came up to the hospital to replace me to go home and get some rest after Shanice's doctor's appointment.

I had planned to do some more packing, but I didn't even have the strength in me to try. I put Shanice in her playpen and passed out right there on the bed.

The next thing I was awakened to Martinez shaking me and asking me why I'm not at the hospital. I woke up like, What the fuck? I didn't know what the hell was going on the way he shook me. My first instinct was to protect myself because knowing Martinez, I didn't know if he would hug me or hurt me. But I got up to get myself together to go back to the hospital; as I'm standing in front of the mirror brushing my hair, Martinez was standing there looking at me, and out of nowhere, he just hog spit on the side of my face for no reason and spew this is what I think of you. I was stunned and speechless, but that was it for me! I have fucking had enough! He had kicked me down for the last time. The audacity of him to fucking spit on me again. I wanted to put a bullet in him and didn't give a fuck if he was my kid's father at this point. I ran over, grabbed Shanice out of her playpen, and we hauled ass out the front door. I didn't care what was packed or not! He could keep all the rest of that shit. I didn't want anything else from Martinez or that whole fucked up situation. It's over, and there was no turning back for me. Is it funny to me? I rather enjoy my hatred towards him so much more than I ever enjoyed my love for him. Love is temperamental as tiring as it makes demands. Love has used me, changed my mind. But hatred, now, that's something I can use, and Sculpt wield it's hard, or soft; however, I need it. Love with him has humiliated me, but hatred towards him will cradle me."

# Chapter 22:

# FREEDOM

"I was tired of my tears burning up my pillow, and
it feels good not to sleep in wetness anymore."

THEY KEPT ANTHONY in the hospital for two weeks before they released
him to go home with me. We were staying with my mother in her
one-bedroom apartment. I slept on the couch, Shanice slept with my
mother in her bed, and Anthony slept in his playpen. It was not the
most comfortable situation, but anything was better than the mental
hell hole I lived in with Martinez. I didn't care about any of the material luxuries anymore. I just wanted to be independent. I stayed with
my mother for two months when Shanice's visiting nurse found us an
apartment. She felt sympathetic to our living situation and volunteered
to help out. The apartment was not in the projects, but it was Section 8
based Housing, determined through the Housing Authority. The rent
price was chosen based on your income, and since I was only able to
work two or three days a week because of Shanice's illness, they told
me I only had to pay $150 a month. That was music to my ears. Now
I would not have to stress about how I would afford my rent. I didn't
care where it was; as long as it was somewhere I could call my own, I
couldn't be happier.

Honestly, I was torn because I liked living with my mother. She was a great help with the kids so, instead of moving into the apartment right away, I decided to stick around. Not only did I like her being there to help me with the kids, deep down, she was also helping me heal. So, I stayed with her for eight months before entirely moving into my place. By the time we moved in, Shanice was three, and Anthony was three months old. I had been able to get a new car, a new job, and a new attitude, so I felt like my independent, adult self again. Everything seemed to be going pretty well; Shanice even seemed like she was starting to get better. Martinez must've finally realized what he had because he was constantly trying to get back together. But that was the last time Martinez would ever hurt me again. I was done this time, and there was nothing he could do about it.

I even started seeing this guy named Dee that I met at Seaside Park in Bridgeport. I had known of Dee for a while from around the way, but we were never formally introduced. He always knew me as Martinez's wife. He didn't know Martinez, and I have been over for eight months. When I saw Dee in the park, I got a little excited because I always had a secret thing for him. Of course, I would have never admitted it; that would've been stupid of me. He always had a thing for me too. He was never too obvious about it, but I got those silent vibes. I used to catch him looking at me across the room at parties. I always knew that if I wanted to go there, I could. Dee walked up to me with a big grin on his face. "What's up, Mrs. Martinez? How's life been treating you?"

"It's not Mrs. Martinez no more, honey."

"Oh yeah? So, I guess that means I can take you on a date."

I betted my lashes up at him and flirted. "If that is something you been longing to do, then I guess so."

"Let's start tonight."

"Tonight?"

"Yes, tonight."

"OK, then, where to?"

"If you hungry, we can grab something to eat."

"I can eat."

"Alright, cool."

We went out to eat that night and instantly fell for each other. Dee took me everywhere. He would fly us to Vegas, spend weekends in Miami, take cruises, and more. We ate at all the finest restaurants, had thousand-dollar shopping sprees. His money was long. That was the only kind of man that I could date after Martinez; someone with cash. I didn't care how he got it as long as he had it. Martinez spoiled me like no other when it came to money, but I guess it came with a price. Martinez didn't like Dee being around one bit, but who cares? He called a lot, telling me he didn't want another man around his kids. I would laugh at him, saying, "You can't be serious. You never around your kids, so who are you to tell me who can or cannot embrace my babies? "I paid that shit no mind. Martinez knew that I had moved on. He started to back off for the most part, but he would come around or call to apologize once in a while. Martinez would say he knew he was wrong and that he could change. He'd never find anyone like me again blah, blah, blah. It was too little too late for me. "Sorry" just wasn't good enough, especially for the beatings, cheating, and disrespect that he put me through. It happened too often to be a mistake. Then it was repeated just because he felt like hitting on me. There was nothing to convince me that he could change. It is necessary, and even vital, to set standards for my life and the people I allow to stay in it; that's when I found myself moving on.

Dee loved my children. He treated my kids just like they were his own. Dee was always taking them somewhere and doing things with us as a family. He would always sit at the hospital with us when Shanice was admitted for one of her attacks. Dee was so sweet; sometimes, he would even tell me to go home and get some rest for the night and volunteer to stay there with her. By the time I would get back the following day, Dee would still be there. He would bring Shanice's gifts back up to the room. She loved him.

Dee had two children of his own, but he still always accepted mine as though they were his, and I adored Dee for that. It was so refreshing to have him in my life after the turbulent relationship I went through with Martinez. I didn't ever think I would survive it, but I did. It had been such a long time since I felt like this. My kids were doing well; I worked, had my place and a car, and it felt great. I felt like a woman in control – I could come and go as I pleased and do what I wanted when I wanted. Life was good. The past was behind me, and the possibilities for my future were endless. I was in love with the new me and promised myself to never let yesterday use up my joy for today.

# Chapter 23:

## SCREAMING

"They must not know my agony and despair. I can't let them see my wounds; I feel alienated from my words. Attacked, silenced, and ignored. I'm listening to those scary voices coming from my heart and letting out through my guts...I feel like I'm cursed."

A YEAR PASSED; Anthony had turned one, and Shanice had just turned four. My father had taken Anthony from me to help take the load off. It was difficult lugging two kids back and forth to the hospital, so I was grateful. Luckily, Shanice seemed to be getting much better. She had stopped going in and out of the hospital so frequently. It had been about a month since Shanice had been to the emergency room. After the second time, her little lungs collapsed, and she almost lost her life. I thought, "How much more could my baby possibly take? How much more could I take?"

The only problem we had now was the medication Shanice took; it made her hair fall out and took away her appetite. She would only eat certain things, so her doctor suggested putting her on PediaSure every day, along with her regular diet. The following winter, it was the end of February, Shanice had a follow-up appointment with her doctor. She was amazed at how Shanice was doing. Dr. S. was telling me how great she looked and that her lungs sounded good. Dr. S. said that eventually, her hair would start growing back once they lowered her steroid dosage. I left the doctor's office with a smile, and Shanice was all giggling. My sister Keisha had picked us up, and we went for ice cream. When we left the ice cream parlor, we went over to see my mother. We were there for a few hours, and I noticed that Shanice had grown quiet. There was something different about her from when we first came from the doctor.

I said, "Shy-Shy, you OK, baby?"
She whispered, "Yes."
I said, "Are you sure?"
She said, "Yes, mommy," and sat on the couch. I sat beside her and said, "Shanice," she turned to me, "let mommy smell your breath. "When Shanice started to get sick, she had a funny smell on her breath. It was a very distinct, stinky smell, an indicator for when she was about to have a severe attack. My heart started pounding deep inside. I grew terrified; something inside me didn't feel right. I looked over at Keisha and said, "Her breath smells. "We all knew what that meant.

I started to give Shanice an early treatment with the machine and a dose of her steroids. Keisha and my mom started playing with her, but she wasn't even in the mood for that. Her energy was low. I told my mom I think it's time for us to head home so Shanice could get some rest, so Keisha and her husband said they would bring us home. On our way there, Keisha's husband was trying to put a smile on Shanice's face, but she was so sad for some reason. She wasn't trying to play with anyone, not even me.

That whole evening, I built walls around me to block out the heavy feeling of sadness building up inside me. I fixed Shanice a snack and bathed her. I asked her if she wanted to watch a movie with mommy. She said yes and asked if we could lie in my bed. I said, "Of course, sweetheart, but before we lie down, you have to take another treatment. "With no problem, she put the medication in the tube and turned on the machine. I looked at her and smiled. I just stared at her, thinking if something ever happened to her, I would die.

I went into my room to put the movie in the DVD player then walked back into her room to see how she was doing. She looked at me and said, "See, mommy, I'm almost finished with my medicine." I started laughing because she said it so cute. I spoke with a smile, "Yep, baby, you're almost done."

Then she said, "Yup, mommy, now it's movie time!" I said, "Yes, baby, it's movie time." Shanice and I lay in the bed and started watching the Lion King, her favorite because she loved all the singing. Shanice was in love with music. She loved Usher; he was her favorite artist. She also liked Mariah Carey. Shanice always used to say Mariah was her mother because they had the same type of hair. I used to laugh because I thought that was so cute of her. Shanice fell asleep during the movie, so I put her in her bed for the rest of the evening. I turned off the T.V. and went to sleep. Around 3 AM, Shanice woke up screaming. She walked into my room holding her stomach, saying, "Mommy, my tummy hurts. Mommy, my tummy hurts." Immediately I noticed her struggling to breathe, so I put her on the machine and called 911 as we waited for the ambulance. Shanice was on top of my bed, just screaming in pain about how bad her tummy hurt. I said, "OK, let mommy rub your tummy." When I pulled up her shirt, I saw that her chest was caving in deeply. I could fit my whole fist in. That's when I knew she was in trouble. I was so scared; all I could do was wonder what was going on, and it seemed like the ambulance was taking forever. I didn't understand why they couldn't get here any faster.

It took over 15 minutes for the E.M.T. to get to my house, but it felt like a lifetime. I called my mom and sisters and even Shanice's dad to let them know what was going on.

On our way to the hospital, the E.M.T.'s started to work on Shy-Shy. They called ahead to the E.R. department to let them know that they were coming in with a child with severe respiratory problems. We got to the E.R. in no time. As they rolled Shanice into the back, I saw my family pulling in also. I stayed with my daughter, holding her hand and trying to comfort her. The doctors asked me what had happened to lead up to this point, and all I could say was "nothing." Everything had seemed fine when she went to the doctor's earlier today. I told them how Dr. S. said Shanice was doing so well. I was the confused one; I could not understand what had happened. The E.R. staff called for a specialist who, of course, was Dr. Zen. He came in and looked at me with the most fucked up look on his face like I had done something wrong. He asked me to step out of the room so they could tube Shanice. They said they had to do it because she was having too much trouble breathing on her own.

I looked at my baby and said, "Mommy is coming right back, sweetheart. I'm going to be right outside the door." Shanice looked at me and said, "Mommy, don't leave me, mommy, please don't leave." I felt my heart drop into my chest. I held Shanice's hand and said, "Mommy is not leaving you. I will be right near the door."

She said, "You promise?"

"Yes, I promise. Mommy will never leave you."

I went into the waiting room where my family was and started letting them know what was going on. As I was sitting there talking with the family, a priest approached us and asked if we were the family of Shanice?

I jumped up and said, "Yes, I'm her mother. And these are my sisters and mom."

The priest looked at me with pain in her eyes and asked, "Can I talk to you guys?"

I said, "Yes… is something wrong?"

The priest said, "Yes, something went wrong while they were working on your child. Shanice went into cardiac arrest when they were tubing her."

"What? Is she OK?" I asked in a panic.

She put her head down. "Well, they had to resuscitate her, and it took about 5 minutes to get her heart beating again."

The priest told us if there was anything, we needed not hesitate to call her. Not long after, Dr. Zen came down to where we were. He was trying to figure out what had gone wrong. He told us that Shanice's condition was so bad that they would have to transfer her to Yale-New Haven Children's Hospital. I didn't mind that because Yale is an excellent hospital for children. I rode in the ambulance with Shanice to Yale Hospital. It took about 25 minutes for them to get her ready. When we got there, we headed up to the I.C.U., where Shanice remained for the next six days. Everyone was there; even Dee stayed there with my family and me the whole time. Dee didn't leave me alone, not once, and I needed all the support I could get because I was in denial of what was happening to my baby.

# Chapter 24:

# TICK-TOCK

"One always has to wait until the sugar completely melts,
and the memory dies, the wound scars over and over, then the
sunsets, but the unhappiness never lift and remains forever."

THE WHOLE TIME we were at Yale-New Haven Hospital, I felt like I was
in a horror film. Everything moved in slow motion; we never quite
knew what was going on. It was as if everything that happened during
that time moved in beats. Tick tock, tick tock To make sense of it all, I
kept a diary of the news as it came in.

## DAY 1

The doctors tell me how Shanice lost a lot of oxygen to the brain,
and she is not breathing on her own right now. Then they tell me
Shanice's condition does not look promising, and she's not doing well.

I was not trying to hear what the doctors are saying. I'm was in
complete denial.

## DAY 2

Shanice's condition is still the same; she's not responding to any medication, tests, or anything. I sat beside her bed all day just talking to her, holding her hands, rubbing her head, and asking God to please let her respond to me. My heart is breaking into millions of pieces. I keep thinking, why is this happening to her? She's just a baby. I would do anything to trade places with her. She has her whole life ahead of her.

Please, God, let my baby live.

## DAY 3

The doctors want to talk to me in private. We went into this big board room.

The doctors and I and the minister of my grandmother's church sat down at the table, and the minister held my hand. Right then and there, I knew they were about to give me bad news. I just sat there with open ears. The doctor said, "Ms. Johnson, it is not going to be easy for me to tell you this, but Shanice is permanently brain dead. Shanice will never be Shanice again, and there is nothing more that we can do."

I sat there quietly with streams of tears rolling down my face. It felt like a knife just stabbed me right in my chest. I couldn't breathe.

Then the doctor said something that stopped me from breathing.

"You're going to have to say your last goodbye."

A sledgehammer knocks me across my head. I feel my whole body go numb.

I cannot even begin to comprehend what these people are telling me. It's like I'm in a nightmare, but I'm awake.

That would be one of the hardest things I would ever have to do.

How could they even suggest that I pull the plug on my child?

As I walked out of the room to deliver my family the horrible news, guess who decides to show up after three days? Martinez, with a woman on his arms who I had confronted a while back about their relationship together. She had repeatedly told me, "no, nothing was going on between the two." I guess the truth always comes out when you least expect it.

I thought this was disrespectful for him to bring her to the hospital, as my child was on her death bed. But to add fuel to the flame, Martinez decided to announce with excitement that this chick was pregnant with his child, and it was a girl, and they were thinking about naming her, Shanice.

I stood there in shock like I was in the Twilight Zone. What type of shit is that to say to me after the three days of hell that I just went through? Then he pops up with this disrespectful bitch talking about having a baby and possibly naming her after my daughter. I was about to lose my mind up in there. The expression on my face let my family know I was about to blow. I felt like someone had just lit my body on fire. That shit was a slap in my face. Dee didn't like it at all either. Everyone noticed that I was about to explode, so Rev. Ash told them the bad news before I could say anything. I just walked out of the room and went outside to get some fresh air.

## Day 4

I still don't have the guts or the strength to pull the plug on my baby. I ask the doctor to please give me one more day. I guess I was hoping for a miracle that Shanice will pull through this.

I keep saying to myself, "I can't do this, I can't do this." Dee tries to encourage me to be strong.

My mom and sisters are crying. We are all heartbroken. I feel mentally destroyed because the decision is all on me.

## Day 5

I still can't muster up the strength to do it. I ask the doctor to please bear with me; I'm just not ready to let go of my child yet. She says she understands and hugs me. She looks at me weirdly and says, "Can I ask you a question? Would you like an autopsy done on Shanice?" Tears start pouring out of my eyes. I sob out, "No, please don't cut open her body. Just please leave my baby alone. Please… this is hard enough on me." I'm walking back and forth, up and down the hallway, punching myself in the head,

Why Lord?

Why me?

Why Shanice?

Why this, God?

Please give me some answers. A sign, Lord!

Help me out; I'm sorry for everything I've done. Please don't punish me this way; don't take my child away from me. Please, God, don't take my child away from me.

I felt like God wasn't listening, or it was just too late for my prayers, and now He couldn't help me.

Day 6

It's time. I haven't slept in days.

I can't stop crying. My heart is aching.

Dee asks me if I am ready?

I barely force out a "no."

The doctors ask if we should call her father.

I say yes.

The doctors try to get a hold of Martinez, but Martinez never answers. My mother and sister decide they are going to go to his house. When they get their no one is there. Martinez is nowhere to be found. I don't want to torture myself any longer.

I tell Dee it's time. Dee asks if I would mind if he came in there with me. I tell him I would like that.

My sisters, mom, and the rest of my family can't go back into her room with us, so Dee grabs my hand, and we walk to Shanice's bed. Shanice is still in I.C.U., so the doctors pull the curtains around to give us privacy. It seems like the whole staff is in tears at this point. Dee sits down and pulls me down on his lap and puts his arms around my waist, and grasps me so tight, and tells me how much he loves us. I was shaken so bad from fear. The doctors start unplugging the ventilator from Shanice and removing all the tubes. Then they place her in my and Dee's arms. We grabbed her and started hugging her and squeezing her so tight.

I'm telling her how much I love her and what a beautiful daughter she is.

I'm begging her not to leave me.

I can feel myself rocking back and forth.

I am crying and trying to sing to her.

As I see her, she takes her last breath.

Silence..............

## Chapter 25:

# FRANTIC

"Earth has no sorrow that heaven cannot heal. There are many things that we don't want to happen to us, but we have to accept, and things we don't want to know but have to learn, and many people we can't live without, but sometimes we have to let go."

I HEARD THE doctors say, "Ms. Johnson, that's it. She's gone." I was so afraid to let her go. I couldn't let her go. I was not letting her go! I was holding onto her so tight, begging the doctor, "Please don't take her away from me." I kept yelling, "Please don't take her... please don't take her out of my arms. Please."

I couldn't stop begging them to get away from me and to let me keep my child. They finally pried her out of my arms, and Dee just grabbed me as I fell to the floor. Dee picked me up and carried me out of the hospital as I screamed, "Please give me my baby back." Dee finally got me in the car and took me to my mom's house, where everyone else was headed. When we pulled up to my mom's house, I felt like I just wanted to die, and as we were going in, I saw Martinez come out of nowhere. He looked at us and said, "Why you're not at the hospital?" I had no words for him. I just charged at him and started hitting him, screaming, Shy-Shy died less than an hour ago!"

Martinez just fell to the porch on his knees, in shock and devastated. Dee proceeded to walk me into the house, laid me down on my mother's bed, and didn't leave my side the whole night. The next day I couldn't move. I just stayed in bed. My family and friends were coming in and out, trying to comfort me. Everyone was very supportive. I was down for days, but I knew I had to get up and make funeral arrangements. No mother should ever have to bury their child. To make matters worse, news reporters were in front of my mother's house daily because Dr. Zen had called Child Protective Services again on me because Shanice had gone into cardiac arrest. I didn't want to leave my house as reporters kept harassing me, asking all these questions about Shanice and how she died. I couldn't believe it! I was so upset! I knew something was wrong when D.C.F. came up to Yale to visit Shanice, but I didn't think anything of it because they didn't come back. I guess they were respecting my privacy and understood what I was going through. I don't think I would have said more than two words to them anyway had they asked me many questions, but I was wrong about them. The news reporters were there trying to put a spin on my situation, turning it into a headline story saying, Another Child Dies in D.C.F. Care. Because at the beginning of that year, four children had died that were investigated by D.C.F., and since Dr. Zen had brought D.C.F. into our lives before, they said the death was because of D.C.F.'s misjudgment.

It didn't matter that Shanice's death was from entirely different circumstances. They still accused me of neglect over and over again. Word had spread all over the city that my child died under D.C.F.'s care for medical negligence. It was overbearing torture. I was so hurt and embarrassed it ran on the news every single day. They made me seem like I killed my child. Everyone had something to say. I felt like everywhere I went, people were pointing at me, whispering under their breath.

"That's the girl who killed her child." I wish people would realize that two-thirds of all gossip is not valid, and the other third is a gross exaggeration. I felt like a direct target. You have to be little to belittle someone else. I cannot stop the gossiping by "answering it." A frontal attack upon gossip cause attention to false stories that are being spread, bringing it to the attention of more and more people.

# Chapter 26:

## DEATH IN A REAL WAY

"My eyes grew tearful as I screamed. This could not be as God saw that you were getting tired and whispered, "Come with me." Your little golden heart stopped beating—hard-working hands at rest. God broke our hearts to prove to us; He only takes the best."

**I GENERALLY FELT** that Shanice realized something was genuinely amiss with her that day. Call me insane; however, regardless of how youthful or old an individual is, they know when it's their time, and I think she realized it was her time. There are places in the heart that don't yet exist, and enduring needs to come into it for those spots to open up. My heart opened up like floodgates when Shanice died, and I was defenseless against anything. At any second, I was at risk of breaking into tiny pieces; I needed to hold it together for Shanice, my son, and my family; however, who would hold it together for me?

The reporters were camped outside of my mom's house, just waiting for something to happen. I tried to avoid them for as long as I could, but they were not budging. Finally, I just said, "Fuck it;" I had to leave the house to make the arrangements for my daughter's funeral, and no one was going to stop me from doing that. It was the only thing that I had left to do for her. I had to make sure it was done right. All I wanted to do was give her a beautiful burial.

Martinez and I went to get Shanice's dress from a boutique. I wanted an exquisite dress for her, not something you could find at any store. I must have been sent to that particular boutique for a reason because I found her entire outfit in there. I got her this beautiful cream dress that went down to her knees, some little frilly lace ankle socks, some cream shoes, and a headband to match. We bought the same dress for Shanice's older sister – Martinez's other daughter – because she and Shanice were very close. I knew she would want to wear something similar to her sister. After dress shopping, I was drained. It had taken so much out of me picking out a dress for my daughter's funeral.

Burying my child was never something I thought I would ever have to do. I had no idea how I was going to make it through this whole process. I still had to go over to the funeral home to bring Shanice's outfit and finalize the details, but I was too upset to go straight to the funeral home. So I just waited for a few hours to pull myself back together. I know a thousand words won't bring her back. I've tried. Neither will a million tears, and pain is an understatement in what I feel. Nobody gets ready for this. It's going to be so hard to comprehend that Shanice is no longer here; my grief is the price I have to pay for her love. Around six that evening, my daughter's Godmother and I went down to the funeral home to bring Shanice's clothes and pay for the remaining fees. I had planned on getting her dressed and doing her hair myself. But as soon as I got to the steps, I just froze. I could not walk through those doors. I couldn't do it. Just the thought of seeing Shanice lying in that room to get her dressed for the last time to say goodbye to her forever was just too painful to do. I just stopped and turned back toward the car. I was crying all the way home. I kept beating myself up inside; I could not help but think that I should have listened to myself and had more tests run on her.

Shanice's Godmother dropped me off at my mother's house and went back to the funeral home to get Shanice dressed. I don't know how she did it; I know I would have broken down if I had gone in that room. I already felt numb, and the slightest thing would make me lose it. When her Godmother returned to the house, she strolled into my mom's room, appearing as though she had been crying. I was lying across the bed in a daze. She looked at me and choked out, "She looks beautiful, just like if you had dressed her yourself. "I couldn't even look at her. I turned my tear-stained face away as I felt more water start to well up. I didn't want to hear anything else about this nightmare. I just wanted to wake up and for it to be over. I needed my little girl back and everything back to normal. To hold her in my arms again, tell her I love her, and hear her voice once more. That was all I wanted, and the only place I was able to talk to her, where I was able to find a moment of peace, was when I was asleep – so that's what I did. I went to sleep.

Forty-eight hours later, after lying in my mother's bed without interruption, I was rudely awakening to my painful reality. It was time for the funeral. I was trying to get myself together. I had been dreading this day, and I was hoping that I would realize this was all a bad dream when I woke up, and Shanice would be here with me, grinning her lovely grin telling me how she felt better today. My brother Tee had been in jail through this whole tragedy. I was kind of sad that he would not be able to be with us for the funeral, but somehow my sisters got him released just in time. That was an extremely decent thing the Department of Corrections did for our family. They didn't have to let him out, but they arranged it because of our tragedy. When Tee saw me, he held onto me so tight and kissed me on my head. He assured me with a sense of security that we were going to pull through this together. With him there and the rest of our family, it made me feel like I had support. I was cheerful Tee could be there for this. It showed me that even though he had consistently been in and out of prison and utilized and sold drugs didn't mean he didn't love and care about his family. We were tight like that. We always looked out for each other, no matter what.

We made the arrangements for the viewing and burial services to be all on the same day. I would not have made it through a two-day service. The limos had arrived, and everyone was ready to go. As the time came closer and closer, I, Dee, and all the children got in the family car. When we arrived at the church, Martinez was already there. There had to be over 300 people there. I was amazed to see how she had touched so many lives to be such a young child. Shanice gained lots of attention from her exposure to the United Way; some of the people from there were at the funeral and a few nurses and doctors from Bridgeport and Yale-New Haven Hospital. All of my family and friends, along with Martinez's family and friends, were there as well. Shanice had a lot of people who loved and adored her.

As I walked into the church, I started to get hot. I felt like I could not breathe like someone had put a plastic bag over my head. I started getting closer towards the casket when I felt my knees shaking. Every step I took grew heavier and heavier like bricks were stacked on top of my feet. My son Anthony was running down the aisle, pulling on my dress and saying to me, "Shy-Shy is sleeping." I just needed air at that point. The room started to spin, and I started gasping for air, but I couldn't find it. All of a sudden, I just fell hard onto the floor, and everything went black.

Dee picked me up and carried me back to the family car. I was in complete shock, and no one knew what to do, so they called 911. I just felt dead within. I had no feeling in my legs and, unable to regain my composure, My chest felt like it was caving in because I had to keep gasping for air. When the ambulance came, they gave me oxygen and checked all my vitals. They inquired about whether I suspected I would have the strength to make it through the rest of the service. I told them, "Yes, I had to do it for Shanice."

I didn't go back into the church.

I stayed in the car lying in Dee's arms until the service was over and it was time to go to the burial site. When the car pulled up, I froze. I could not move; I couldn't take this anymore. My heart couldn't handle it, so I didn't get out of the car. There was no way I could say bye to my baby. How can any parent say goodbye to their child? This was a

nightmare that I would never wish on anyone, not even my worst enemy, and I would never be the same. I felt like I was already dead. And
what was left living, I wanted to kill. Death is not the hardest thing to
deal with in life. The hardest thing is having the courage to continue to
get up and live while everything else inside you is dead; that is death in
a real way – when you are living, but you feel nothing inside.

# Chapter 27

# SAME OLE' SAME OLE.'

"After all, we can't expect things to ever be any different from this commonly held opinion that our successes
or failures in life are determined by our decisions."

IT HAD BEEN a little over a month since Shanice passed away. I had gone
back to stay at my mom's house. I just didn't want to be alone. It was
and still is a nightmare to me. All I did was lie in bed. It seemed like
I could not pry myself from it. Sleep was my comfort. Everyone kept
trying to get me out of the house to cheer me up, but I was not in the
mood. I didn't have the energy; I didn't want people asking me if I was
OK, and I didn't want to pretend like I was OK. For a few days, Dee
had gone out of town, so he rented a car for me to pick him up from
LaGuardia Airport since his truck was in the shop. He also thought it
was a good idea to get me out of the house for a day. I asked my sister
Keisha to ride with me for the company. She agreed, so we packed up
my son Anthony and went to pick up Dee from the airport. As we
were approaching Fairfield County, a tractor-trailer started merging
over into our lane. There was a car on my blind side, so I could not
move over. I started honking my horn at the trucker to get his attention. When he finally saw me, it was too late. The trailer hit us and

hooked our car onto it. It started dragging us up the highway, which caused our car to spin around and around, faster and faster. Everything was happening so fast. There was nothing I could do to stop the truck we were going to crash. The trailer swung us out, and we slammed hard against the barrier head-on. The back end of our S.U.V. went up into the air and then came slamming back down, smashing loudly into the ground. For a split second, everything was silent. All I could think about was Anthony in the back seat. I couldn't bear losing another child.

As I started to turn around to see if my son and my sister were OK, my airbag deployed, smacking me in the face, and busted my nose. Blood started pouring out, and before I knew it, I was out cold. When I came to, Keisha was in a panic, shaking me to wake up. I wasn't sure how long I had been out for, but I needed to know if my son was OK. Keisha's knee was stuck in the dashboard, and she could not move, and frantically trying to get loose. I turned to the back seat to check on my baby boy, and he was on the floor clapping his hands and yelling, "Yay, yay!" like he thought we were on an adventure or something. Keisha and I looked at one another with the biggest smiles on our faces. We were just happy that he was OK. When we all walked out of that horrible accident alive, I just knew it was Shanice watching over us, our guardian angel. But it seemed like chaos continued to follow me.

I couldn't get it together. Everything bad you could think of started happening. Things that you would only see in the movies began happening to me in real life. I began to feel like I'm cursed because of all the shit I did when I was growing up. I started leaving the house a little more, trying my hardest to keep my mind occupied with peace and acceptance to overcome Shanice's passing, in attempting to teach myself to survive, live, and dare to confront each day. One day I took Anthony over to visit my sister Sharon, who was having a little barbeque at her house. Everyone was full of joy, standing around, talking and laughing as usual, but all I could think of was getting out of there to keep my mind off Shanice, but before I could say goodbye, two guys that we knew started to fight. We were watching them go at it and had no idea what had started it. One thing led to another, and then someone started shooting at the two guys from another direction. As soon as we heard the gunshots, we all started gathering all the children up before anyone got hurt. A bullet hit one of the fighters, and he ran over towards us as we pushed the children to get in the house. Anthony was at the bottom of the steps in an umbrella stroller, eating an ice cream cone when the injured guy grabbed the back of the stroller with both hands and pushed my son directly in front of him as a shield. I ran over to grab Anthony as the other guy pointed the gun at him. He pulled the trigger, and the gun went off; thank God it didn't hit anyone. My sister Sharon and one of our friends were kicking the guy, screaming and crying to pull my son away from the man, but he had such a tight grip on the stroller it took a few of our friends to help me peel his fingers off the carriage. Then the other guy pulled the trigger again, but luckily the gun jammed.

I grabbed my son, pushed the guy out of the way, and ran into the house with my baby. I had known both of those guys, and one used my son as a human shield. Everyone around the way knew what had just happened to my daughter, and here they were willing to take my son out too. It seemed like death was following my children. But I was not going to let anything happen to Anthony. I would never forgive myself. I couldn't take losing another child; my son suffered minor hearing loss due to the noise of the gun. After that, I kind of fell back from hanging in the projects. I felt it wasn't worth being out there anymore, especially when my son's life had been so close to ending. D.C.F. was still in our lives from all the investigations with Shanice. Somehow, they heard about the shootout involving Anthony, and things were not getting any better as they tried to take my son because of that incident, but they would have to kill me first before they made my child a ward of the state. So, my sister Keisha and I decided that she take permanent custody of Anthony to get them out of my life forever. So, we went down to the court, filed the paperwork, and Anthony started living with Keisha. I thank her every day for that.

After D.C.F. closed the case and Anthony started living with my sister, I should have felt relieved. But I didn't; my body and soul were completely drained. Everything wrong that could happen to a person had happened to me, and it didn't seem like it was not getting any better. I couldn't figure out why so much bad luck was following me. I was mentally and emotionally exhausted. I had no reason to live. That's when I had enough, and I decided I'm better off dead. Dr. James sat there with his mouth wide open. He looked like he was in a trance. It seemed like we had been in his office forever. That had to be the longest hour of my life, but I had let it all out. I knew that it was the only way he was going to release me from this crazy house. I had told him everything. And the truth is it felt good.

He sat back and looked up at the clock. "Looks like we lost track of time," he said. I looked up at the clock and noticed we were almost an hour over my session time. I didn't care. Where did I have to go? All I was concerned about was telling him enough so that he would understand how I ended up here. I knew that once anyone heard even half of my story and all the bullshit I have been through, they would understand exactly why I tried to kill myself. Everyone has their breaking point.

I looked at Dr. James's desk and saw the picture of his three kids: by the look on his face, you can tell he was thinking about them, wondering how he would react if he had lost one of them. I could tell his heart was filled with compassion for me. His tone of voice even got softer. I was no longer a patient in his eyes; I was a friend. I was now someone he wanted to help.

He asked me, "How do you feel now? Do you still want to kill yourself?"

I took a deep breath and shook my head.

"What is different now?" he asked.

I had to pause for a minute because that was not something I had thought about; what was different now? I guess I was different.

There isn't anything that can make you appreciate life more than a failed suicide. Maybe there was a reason I was here. I never really looked at life that way. I was always concerned about what we had or didn't have. About what a man could do for me; how much money someone had. I was never apprehensive about things that mattered, like Love, trust, faith, and God.

The psych ward made me realize that I am not crazy. I am fully aware of what I am doing and what is going on around me. After being around people like Milly, I know what crazy is for real; that is not me. I said to him, "Now, I don't want to kill myself. Yes, I am still in a lot of pain from my daughter's death, but I know I have to keep on for my son and my family. Do I want Shanice back? Yes, more than I have ever wanted anything. But I know now that killing myself won't bring her back. It will just hurt more people. And I don't want anyone else to hurt. I just want to start healing."

A smile spread across Dr. James's face. It was the first time I saw him break his serious poker look. I knew that meant I was going to be out of here soon. All I needed was for him to write a good recommendation for my doctor, and I would be out. I wasn't sure if I even believed I was better. I knew I was good enough to go home and feel better on a soft mattress with sheets on the bed. I knew I would love to take a hot, private shower and do something to my hair. Those were the things that I was sure of – but Dr. James didn't need to know that. I watched him scribble some things into my chart and then fold it closed in front of me.

"I think you are ready to go home," he said.

I stared at him blankly, like I wasn't sure what he said. I responded so I wouldn't miss the moment.

"I will get this report over to your doctor. I will see if we can get you released by tomorrow." I felt a slight smile creep on my face. It was the closest thing to a smile I could push out. The next day Dee came to the hospital to pick me up. It was finally over. I was out of the hospital and ready to start healing.

*Chapter 28:*

# THE CRASH

"A person's ability to choose is a privilege and a responsibility. Sometimes our wrong turns can be detrimental to our well-being and put us in danger of losing ourselves indefinitely."

IT HAD BEEN two years since Shanice passed away, and I was still trying to claim ignorance. It felt like my brain was pulling pranks on me. Anthony was still with my sister Keisha, and I was back in my apartment, alone. I kept my mental stability by discovering approaches to numb myself by becoming inebriated, getting high off Ecstasy, and partying. Martinez was locked up. The feds finally caught up with him and sentenced him to 20 years in federal prison three months after Shanice's passing, and it seems like as days, weeks, and months go by, drama still follows me. I was still getting into fights. My sister Sharon and I had got accused, arrested, and burned with a chemical substance and went to trial for a crime we didn't commit. But with God's help and over twenty thousand dollars paid, we regained our freedom after they saw our innocence.

My relationship with Dee was rocky. However, through my entire misdemeanor, he stuck with me and still treated me like a queen, and would still go the extra mile to see me smile. I can admit he was my rock, there is no denying that, but our relationship turned sour because he couldn't remain morally upright. That was a significant problem for me and that was what placed a damper on our relationship. I couldn't understand why I kept going through this with every man I dated. I couldn't win for losing. I thought that Dee would be more sensitive after all I've been through, but instead, he added to my pain. I and Dee had been together four years, and the love I have for him has been phenomenal and filled with passion. This however made me devastated when I got to know about Dee's cheating habit.

I couldn't help but think about his cheating behavior and why he chose to hurt me. I wondered how he could be sleeping around with other women when he's with me damn near all day, every day.

This was more than I could take, so I decided to move on, because I didn't want to go through any more drama from Dee or anyone else, hence, I called it quits. Nobody likes an emotional cheat; however, most emotionally bankrupt individuals will cheat if they know they will get away with it. Everyone was born a sinner, however, whilst growing up, the degree of the sins differs, some sin more, others, less. As days go by I continued to ponder and ask myself the reason he cheated. Did he cheat because I wasn't paying more attention to what he was missing rather than what he has? All the questions that cross my mind weren't questions I had answers for. However, I figured at this point that being single is better than being lied to, cheated on, and disrespected. These were values I can't negotiate for anything.

Dee apologized and pleaded for me to stay, saying he acted immaturely. He said he wanted to become a changed man and that he would never hurt me again. But I now know better. I understand that that is what they all say when they get caught. It was just a little too late. I still loved Dee. He called every day, but I just ignored his messages. He had done more than enough to my emotions; hence, I was ready to move on. A week has passed without any word from Dee. I was relieved; well, not really! I started having a problem getting used to being alone in the house and this made me feel Dee's absence very much. But I remained steadfast in my decision, refusing to talk to him. The thought of cheating remained fresh in my mind, thus making me detest being with him. However, now that he was gone, I felt lonely than ever. I was tired of lying around, so I decided to get in the shower, get dressed so I could get out of the house before I start having flashbacks. I left the bathroom door open since I was home by myself, just if the phone rang or someone knocked on the door. As I was in the shower, I suddenly heard some glass shatter. I hopped out of the shower dripping wet, and I wrapped a towel around me to see what was going on. As I got closer to the kitchen, I could see my window shattered and Dee trying to climb through. I screamed, "Dee, what the hell are you doing?" I tiptoed over and opened the back door, so he could come in instead of getting cut by the glass. I didn't know what was going on and I wasn't sure if he was knocking. As I opened the door, he walked in and grabbed me by the neck, and my wet feet slipped from under me, and I hit the floor landing on my back. Dee stood over me, breathing hard like a wild dog, spittle dripping from his mouth.

He started hurling punches into the floor to avoid punching me, saying, why you hurt me. "I trusted you completely, and I was repaid for it by getting hurt." Besides me leaving Dee let's just say I wasn't perfect either as trust starts with truth and ends with truth. But in no way I was honest with Dee as I totally betrayed his trust and completely violated it. When you hurt someone, or hurt people, it obviously will have a ripple effect, so never start this chain of hurt. And to me, it was a lesson learned on both sides.

Still, on top of me, Dee started choking me with complete rage. I was kicking my feet and gasping for air, but it seemed like, with every breath I took, he just squeezed harder. I was scared out of my mind. Dee never hit me before; we barely argued, it was not his attitude to hit a woman, but my disrespect led him to become a different person. My mind raced, thinking of what I could say to calm his raging emotions down but fortunately, at that point, Dee came back to his senses, realizes what he was doing, and finally freed his hands from around my neck. I've never been so scared in my entire life. I was dazed and confused because this man was nothing but good and supportive to me our entire relationship. So why is this happening? I asked myself in confusion. I was however relieved to hear the cops banging on the door. I guess one of my neighbors heard the noise and called 911. I've never been so happy to see the police in my life. When they burst into the door, Dee knew it was over; one cop asked if I was OK, while the other officers were putting handcuffs on Dee. The cops had my whole street blocked off. In case Dee tried to run, but there was no escaping, there were cops everywhere, and at this point, I couldn't be happier to see them.

I was shaken up that I could barely talk. When the ambulance got to my house, I refused to go to the hospital. I was so over hospitals after Shanice had died, and I was too embarrassed. I didn't want the media all up in my business again and people gossiping about Dee trying to hurt me, so E.M.T. just checked my vitals and cleaned up my bruises. I had lacerations around my neck and some marks on my legs and arms. The cops still tried to convince me to go to the hospital for medical attention, but I still refused. I did not want to leave my house. I could not believe Dee would ever try to do something like this to me. I asked myself-Was he going to take my life? I don't know, but I will say two wrongs don't make it right.

Dee, the man who loved me unconditionally, got charged, and the state took over the case due to the nature of the crime. Now Dee would have to face whatever was coming to him. He ended up receiving two years in jail for this crime. It's been months since Dee had got incarcerated, and I am still in shock of what happened but still in love, and I think about Dee all the time. I feel more alone than ever, especially with Shanice gone and Anthony living with Keisha. I was in such a deep depression I had no idea what to do with myself. I didn't want to eat or sleep. I just wanted to be numb to the pain. So, I went back to partying every night, from Sunday to Sunday, and became a heavy drinker. I would have a glass of wine for breakfast, a Patron for lunch, and a Hennessey by nightfall.

Bridgeport wasn't doing it for me anymore either. I had too much bad luck there, so I felt it was time to make myself known to some new stomping grounds. I started hanging out in New York City. The city becomes like my second home. I was meeting all types of people. My girlfriends knew damn near everyone important in the industry, and I was right aboard to be a part of that whole scene. All of my friends were beautiful and exotic-looking women. Everywhere we went, we were the center of attention, and we loved it. I was always at the hottest parties and was kicking it with some of the biggest stars out. The industry is something else. When they say the phrase sex, drugs, and rock and roll, they are not playing. These parties would have so many drugs; it seemed like it was legal. That's when I was introduced to Ecstasy for the first time, and life for me began to grow out of control.

Some of my new connections in N.Y. even introduced me to the business of credit card schemes. It was easy. I was taught how to make fake credit cards and take orders. I took orders from people for big-ticket items – from big screen T.V. to jewelry, furniture, and more. It didn't matter what you wanted, I would order whatever, and I would charge them a meager price. My items were going like hotcakes. The credit card game was good. I was making a couple of thousand dollars damn near every day. It was better than selling drugs. I felt more comfortable doing schemes than being out in the streets all night trying to hustle drugs. It was still a risk with the law, but I was slick with it. The money I was making from the credit cards had me living fabulous. A lot of that money was just feeding my alcohol and pill addiction. I was still partying like a rock star and had been doing this credit card shit for about four years now, but I was tired of the game, so I decided to give a few more orders than I was out. I had just placed an order for some computers for overnight delivery. Overnights were the best. They came on time, and the money was ready on arrival. I waited at my staged house for all my deliveries all day, but the FedEx truck never showed up. I was pissed! I was looking to get my money from that delivery, and there had never been a late delivery. Usually, when I placed my orders, I would get them the next day with no problem. But the order never showed up. I got a little suspicious, so I called the company to see what was up. They told me that the delivery truck had gotten into an accident, but they would have my packages sent to me first thing in the morning.

The next day, around 10 AM, the white delivery truck pulled up to my house with the computers as promised. I was extremely happy because my greedy ass wanted my money. As I was signing for the package, I happened to look over at the delivery truck and notice that it did not say FedEx on it. I could have kicked myself in the ass because I knew it was a setup right then and there. I realized that it was too late. I had already signed for the package, which meant that I might as well have just signed a letter that said, "I'm guilty."

Cops started jumping out of the white truck from every direction. The cop with the package started reading me my rights as the other officers ran past me, pushing in my front door and searching the house. Luckily, I was smart enough not to leave any merchandise at my staged home. They didn't find anything, but they did have my signature on that delivery slip, and that was all they needed.

Down at the station, the detective told me they had been investigating me for a long time. There was no time for me to cry now. I was caught! I took the rap for everything, and I had a good time while it lasted, but now it was over. I called my homegirl and told her to go to my house and get some money to bond me out. I told her where I hid my stash, and she came down to the jail and bonded me out. I had to pay $2,500 to get out. With all the money I had made, that was nothing to me. I don't know why he did it, but my dad paid my lawyer fees, and I thanked him for that. I had to go back and forth to court for six weeks. They gave me a suspended sentence, and I got three years' probation and had to pay $10,000 restitution. I got another police record. Ughhhh!

I was fucked! I had quit my job because the money was so good from the credit cards, but there was no more money coming in after being caught, so the money I had put up was running dry. However, it didn't help because I was blowing most of it on alcohol and drugs. No matter what I did, I couldn't shake my Ecstasy habit; I didn't know what I was going to do. My drug habit started getting out of control. I was worshipping those pills. I had to have them. Almost everyone was taking them, so I didn't feel like it was a drug. There were so many kinds, from the humble aspirin lookalike to the multi-colored king-sized triple-deckers. They would stimulate and soothe me all in one. I took them to keep the demons away. I had to take them daily because I had to take another one right away to avoid being sick once my high started wearing down. UGHHHH! It was so easy to get thousands of pills, but it was hard to get one single remedy on how to stop that shit. I wanted to quit, but my body needed them. I was like a crackhead, and there was nothing anyone could say or do to get me to stop popping those pills.

One night that shit caught up with me; I had taken my daily dosage of Ecstasy. Suddenly, my whole body started shaking out of control; after a few moments, foam-like substances started emanating from my mouth, then I hit the floor. Fortunately, one of my friends was in the house with me, she heard a loud noise and ran into the bedroom to see what was going on. Out of intense fear, she started screaming out and she immediately called 911. It took E.M.T. about 10 minutes to get to my house, and then they rushed me to the hospital.

When they arrived, the doctors took me right in, and the E.M.T.'s informed them of a possible overdose. They immediately started pumping my stomach. It was indeed a terrible feeling, but I was glad to get the whole shit out of my system. I thought I was going to die, and with the path, my life was on at that point, it looked exactly like that was going to happen. The above story of my life just shared now is typical of some folks out there. They are involved in drugs, partying, fraudulent activities, and a whole lot of despicable activities that are capable of putting their lives in absolute jeopardy. Research reveals that peer pressure and destructive association, lack of purpose, and the inability to discover their potentials have been responsible for these unhealthy behaviors.

Everyone created by God has been created to fulfill a purpose in this world. However, without purpose and an understanding of the reason for existence, abuse is inevitable. Lack of potentials and purpose discovery will make an individual believe that life is all about having fun, partying, having sex with multiple partners, lounging, engaging in drug addiction, and the likes, thus wasting invaluable time and resources for unprofitable ventures when others are busying making impacts, surpassing the norm and breaking the jinx of mediocrity in their generation.

# Chapter 29:
## THE RE-BIRTH

"Once you've admitted to yourself, you're
on the wrong path, decide how you're
going to get back on track."

**MY LIFE WAS** going downhill. I hadn't seen my son in months. I was on the verge of losing my apartment because I had run out of money. I had no job; I barely ate, and I didn't give a damn about anything. After Shanice's passing, it was hard to get my life back on track; my life had completely fallen apart. I had to stop the bullshit. Lying on that hospital table, looking up at those bright lights burning into my eyes, was my wake-up call.

Growth is a painful process. Everything I've done was something I chose to do. Some people don't want to believe that. But if you decide to go down that wrong path, then you will find

yourself in a world of trouble. Life is what you make of it. To change your life, you need to change your priorities, and it was time I took that advice. Even the knowledge of my fallibility cannot keep me from making any more mistakes. If you have made mistakes, there is always another chance for you to make a fresh start at any moment you choose. You can start over whenever you want, any day, at any moment, but you need to commit to consciously reduce your mistakes, by mastering your weakness and concentrating on your strengths.

You may wonder how I can leave all my problems behind if they are always in my face? To be hopeful in bad times is not foolish. I have seen and experienced the most exceedingly awful, and now I need to turn around and stroll the correct way. All it took was a life-undermining reminder, a modest quantity of assurance, and ravenous confidence towards my central goal.

I left that emergency room a changed lady. I realized that there was no chance I could return to the life I was living. However, because I endured this slip-up doesn't mean I will survive the following. I understood that even though Shanice was gone, I still had to be a mother for Anthony. I had to be there as a sister to Keisha, Sharon, and Tee. I was still my mother's daughter, my father's girl, and most of all, God's child. This was the time to change my life and begin on a clean slate.

After putting the drugs behind me, I started to pursue my music career as a hip-hop artist. Something I have been longing to do since I was 14 years old, but my mind was on other things, of course. When I got locked into the business, I took the music industry by storm. I was in the studio day in and day out, recording song after song, working with various producers, and doing a lot of traveling, trying to make a name for myself. I even moved to Manhattan, New York, California, and Atlanta, to pursue this music thing. I pursued this goal with all I had in me for ten years, but I endured too many ups and downs and decided it was finally time for me to put the mic down. As a female hip-hop artist at that time, it was hard trying to get into the industry and break into the mainstream, especially if you're not screwing your way to the top. The music industry is and can be a cutthroat business; even though I love it with a passion, I felt it was not worth giving up my body or losing my sanity over it. So, I decided to continue writing and write books. Putting pen on paper has always been my God-given potential, and I wouldn't have it any other way. I also ventured a little into some local modeling, nothing major, but it paid the bills.

As days rolled by, I met a new guy; he was a professional basketball player who played for a few teams, but he was retiring from the New York Knicks when we got together. We dated and lived together for over five years; it wasn't the best five and a half, years but we made it that far. This relationship was different because I was helping him overcome a lot of his addictions and demons while I was still fighting mine. But it was fine with me as I stood by his side with unconditional love when no one else did. However, I endured too much verbal abuse in the

relationship due to his addiction to alcohol to remain a couple. Today he has gotten the help he needed and is doing great, with a resolution to put the past behind us and remained good friends, as we went our separate ways.

Connecticut was becoming too much for me. I had lost myself, my child, my mom, who passed away suddenly in her sleep in August 2010, my four-year-old nephew in 2011 from brain cancer, who was like my child, as I held him in my arms and watched him take his last breath. These back-to-back deaths kept sending me back into depression. However, not forgetting all the bad relationships of traumatizing physical, verbal and mental abuse. These incidences made me decide to leave Connecticut in 2013 to North Carolina to stay with my sister Sharon with just two hundred dollars in my pockets.

After all the messed-up decisions with finances, I had nothing by spending stupid and not being financially smart, another lesson learned.

In my first year in N.C., I was homesick, but I decided to stick it out and make the place my new home. In my first few weeks, I could not find a job, but the hustling spirit in me always remain. In the words of Albert Einstein, he stated that "in the middle of every difficulty lies opportunity". I decided to stand and make things happen for myself instead of waiting for a miracle, so I put an Ad on craigslist to clean houses. I knew about this business from my grandmother as that was her occupation throughout her entire life. After my first two calls, I turned it into a business. I started making six hundred dollars a day. I was cleaning homes at first, then expanded and started getting contracts for daycares, private schools, and banks. I'm blessed for those opportunities, but it took a significant toll on my body after a while. No gain without significant pain!

During my first year in N.C., I made a decision not to date again for a while, but I decided to give love another try. I was not looking for an industry guy or a street guy. I just wanted a regular man with a "nine to five" job who would love me and only me, but that was not the case. Mr. North Carolina was younger than me; we had a nine-year age difference. Can you imagine that? But the most amazing thing is that we fell in love instantly. Without further ado, we quickly began a relationship, and also moved in together after two weeks of dating. Our first year was indeed awesome, however, in our second year, we opened a business together, "an in-home daycare,". In our third year of dating, we opened a center together. Amazingly, I transformed this average "nine to five" worker into a business owner and got him out of the corporate world. I gave him the confidence to become a boss, but that was the biggest mistake I could have ever made. As the money rolled in, the immaturity began. What happened to the man I first met?

This man became the most openly disrespectful person I ever met in my life. He was a complete
materialistic, selfish, cheating, and lying man I have ever been with, even the richest man treated me with far more respect than this guy. At least in my past relationships, they tried to hide it, but no, not this one.

In addition to all his misdemeanor, he started bringing women to our place of business and also to our home with the audacity to sleeping with them in our bed. He never allowed me to be around his daughter because he was sleeping with his child's mother, and even spoke ill about me and constantly lie about everything. He would lie when the truth will do. Mr. North Carolina can tell me it is was raining outside; I still wouldn't believe him.

The most heart-breaking is that when I was admitted to the hospital for 28 days fighting for my life and almost died of colon disease, he was barely by my side. When I had to fly back home due to the loss of my father in April 2014 and my grandmother in July 2016, he was far from being supportive.

During the burial of my grandmother that coincided with my birthday, he neither called nor showed up. With this unbelievable attitude of his, his friends were super angry at the way he treated me.

After seven years together, I was fed up and just could not accept any more foolishness and disrespect. All my years of dating this guy turned out to be something different. However, I still tried to stick around because of the business we were building together, and most importantly, I was still in love.

A point came when I had to give up. How do you explain when a person tells you he wants to be single for two years straight while still in a relationship; obviously, there is nothing else to discuss.

After a while, I got so angry at myself for putting up with so much humiliation I endured from Mr. North Carolina, knowing that I deserved better, and not getting any younger (I was in my forties).

In December 2019, I left Mr. North Carolina and refused to continue to be a stranded fool. My brain figured out that it will be sheer foolishness if I continuously wait around for someone else to make me happy, hence I reasoned it out that my happiness is solely dependent on me. By looking foolish and allowing myself to be trampled upon, I know I would never have the possibility of being great and exceptional.

For years it wasn't easy for me to move past all the hurts, pains, and avoidable mistakes that characterized my journey so far. But I was deliberate, to work on myself and to let go of my mistakes and those things I have done and put up with in the past.

Consequently, I must say that this last relationship opened my eyes to the reality of deceptive love and self-consciousness with particular emphasis on an accelerated growth as a result of my previous mistakes and past experiences. However, when the person you love can't love you unconditionally regardless of your misdemeanor, or perhaps your status, it will then be imperative to take a walk.

Dear reader, it is important to understand who you are-your

identity. Once you understand who you are, it would be impossible for anyone to maltreat, abuse, and manhandle you. You are valuable, you are special, you are better than the way they think you are. Jettison that feeling of inadequacy, insecurity, and dependency on your partner for happiness. You deserve to be happy, loved, cherished, and adored unconditionally. However, because you know who you are, what you carry on the inside of you, your purpose, and your God-given destiny, you should not allow anyone to take advantage of you. Remember, a relationship is meant to be enjoyed and not endured for any reason.

# Chapter 30
## THE NEW BEGINNING

To FORGET THE baggage of the past and make some new beginnings, you have to let go of what didn't work, held you back, or feared you in any way, just create room to become a better you.

Today I still suffer from depression. Depression is the most unpleasant thing I have ever experienced sometimes keeps me in such a hard place mentally. It affects my behavior,

motivation, and feelings, making the pain hard to bear because I feel messed up inside. I try not to brood over the loss of my daughter, my nephew, my parents, my past mistakes, all the abuse I endured, and failures as these situations always fill my mind with grief, regret, and depression. But this is the thing about my depression; I had survived everything I've been through, but it is so insidious it compounds me daily and makes it impossible to see the freaking end of it.

Some people will never understand this as Mental illness; and the fact that it lives around us every single day. I have seen it in my family and amongst friends. I'm not grateful for my depression, but honestly, it has made me work much harder, giving me the drive that I need to succeed and to make this illness work and vow not to go through what I have been through ever again. I reminisce and get sad a lot about my parents, and it's funny how things happen when you become an adult.

You finally start to realize that your parents are real humans with flaws and all. Even though my relationship with my parents had a conflict before their passing, it was all because I couldn't change my parents. Still, I had to change myself and allow myself to grow, mature, and develop that healthy communication with them. I started to take my time to honor them no matter what because I didn't want to wait until it was too late. I wish I would have given my parents the same love and understanding that I would have for anyone else at a young age. Now, when I have challenges, I use them as an opportunity for growth; that way, everyone benefits. This is why I left my business relationship with Mr. North Carolina, which hurt me to depart from something I built and loved.

I forgave Mr. Martinez for all the wrongdoing he has done to me in the past, like many things I did not discuss because it is traumatizing. After his release from federal prison, we talked like mature adults as he apologized to me for everything he has put me through. We are now on good terms as he is doing very well for himself and building a great relationship with our son. My son Anthony is now 25 years old; after a few years of counseling together, my son and I now have a great relationship, and there is not a day that goes by without him telling me he loves me.

After nineteen years of separation, I married the man who always put me first, stood by my side, and loved me unconditionally. YES; that is Dee, who apologized to my entire family and me before committing to each other again. When I cried because of him, he felt the hurt more than me because he never had the intention of hurting the most important person in his life.

He did to me with the kind of damage and understands that sometimes sorry is not enough, he has however made extra effort to change for good. We all know that it takes immense strength to say sorry, but it takes a much stronger heart and intentional effort to forgive. Dee assured my family and me that he would change so that he doesn't have to apologize for something like that again. I never thought that we would be married in my wildest dream, but our love for each other never faded through all my relationships. He has been with me through many storms; I

guess you can say no storm has been able to overcome our love. He is a one in a million kind of person and was always there even through our separation. Our trials have tried to weigh us down, but our love for each other has always kept us strong as our problems were interesting challenges. I don't know if I'm still wrong for loving someone who once physically harmed me, or am I'm stupid. Still, all these things constantly go through my head, so why give Dee a second chance when you've not given a second chance to your other relationships?. Well, I did. I think I gave all my previous relationships more chances than they deserve but they never took full responsibility for their wrongs.

A second chance doesn't mean anything if you didn't learn from the first. People who are inconsiderate of your heart and feelings don't deserve you. Part of giving a second chance is taking responsibility for what a person did wrong in the first place. And Dee did just that by putting my feelings first. I now realize the bullshit that I had been going through was not about me. It was about the story, about how I could now say that I lived through it. If I could help one person overcome the demons they were facing in their lives, then everything I had gone through was for a purpose. Not just for me, but for all the pretty girls in the world who have to deal with life's bullshit. Remember, being pretty is an asset, but there is nothing like being a Bad Bitch, a beautiful woman who has control of her own life; who doesn't have to depend on a man for anything; and who carries herself well and knows what she wants.

There isn't anything a man can do for you that you can't do for yourself. Trust me. If you want to avoid the bullshit, I went through with men, and other series of events, take heed. I am telling you from experience. I lived A Pretty Girl's Bullshit. In the end, we all have our own lives to live. Some are cut short too soon but fully lived. Others are lived much longer, yet we soon forget what a blessing it is simply to be alive. We make mistakes along the way and lose focus on what truly makes us happy. It's not about the fine clothes, the expensive cars, or living in luxury; these things create pride, jealousy, and resentment. They make a false impression that others love you. True happiness is in the way a person can positively affect your entire life with joy. It's about knowing you and experiencing the pleasure of being loved and cared for by others!

My life has done a 360 to Maturity. I've made up my mind never to allow verbal, mental, or physical abuse in my life anymore. I made a promise to myself that I will no longer let depression, anxiety, or drugs take over me mentally. Make your life a masterpiece; imagine no limitations on what you can be, have, think, or do.

Dear friends, what are you going through? Have you made series of mistakes just like me? What are the limitations that have crippled you from living your life to the fullest? Why are you still in that pitiable state, calling pity party? Do you think you are finished and you've got no hope?

I have good news for you. No matter the errors or mistakes you have made in the past, you can still bounce back.

So what steps can you take to bounce back?

1.Own your mistakes

Yes, you have to own up to your mistakes. Of course, this part is extremely difficult. Owning up to it is the only way to start the process of bouncing back from whatever mistakes you've made. You have to critically look at the whole situation and accept full responsibility for the wrongs. Don't engage in bulk passing or playing to the gallery. Never make excuses for your misdemeanor. Accept the fact that you've messed up, and make frantic efforts to fix the mistakes.

2. Determine to let it go

You're probably going to feel bad about making mistakes. Sometimes, they might be mistakes you had promised yourself that they won't be repeated. It is however easy to let yourself free fall into the gulf of self-pity, self-doubt, self-pity, and shame but that will not help you in any way. Take out a few moments to reflect and remind yourself that you are human. The point is how do you respond to whatever errors or mistakes you have made? Remember, it is how you respond to the mistakes and how you work towards correcting them is that is important.

Determine with all sense of seriousness to let go of all the mistakes you have made. Make up your mind to stop thinking about the past. Let the past remain past. Focus on your present and of course your incredible future. Let go!

3. Critically analyze the mistake, understand what went wrong, and see it as a learning experience.

You have made mistakes, terrible mistakes, right? Mistakes that you find a bit difficult to forgive yourself. But, you know what? Every mistake you have made if critically analyzed carries along with a potential lesson, and a growth process inherent in it. Once you realize this, it will be a lot easier for you to bounce back, no matter how massive the mistake.

Here are some questions to consider:

What went wrong?

Were you blinded by love that you refused to read the writing on the wall?

Did you trust someone you shouldn't have?

Were you in association with the wrong set of people?

Did you disregard the call to discover your God-given potentials?

Was there an oversight? Where?

Were you immature in handling situations?

What could have been done to prevent this mistake?

4. Implement the lessons learned from your mistakes. After you've analyzed and found what led to the mistake, the next step is to

implement any necessary changes and make a commitment to avoid falling into the same mistake in the future.

Dear reader, it's not the end of the world. Your life is not finished just yet. Get up and begin again with a renewed vigor and commitment to take on life again!

"IF YOUR STRENGTH HAD A PRICE, YOU TOO WILL BE A MILLIONAIRE."

My Children - Shanice & Anthony Martinez

8-23-93 to 3-8-98
R.I.P To My Beautiful Angel - Shanice Ashley Martinez

My parents Yvonne Johnson & Bobby McDaniels
and My grandmother Carrie Johnson better known
as Nana I love and miss you guys very much

**GALE BLAZZE JOHNSON,** Born Gale Lanore Johnson who mostly goes by the name Blazze to many friends and fans. She is Co-Owner of Lamar and Lanore Enterprise's, Lamar and Lanore Publishing Group, Creator of Ashley M. (animated character) and more business adventures to come. She lives in NC with her husband Damon Walker. Where she is also a Master Mindset Life Coach + Grief and Loss. The Autobiography of Gale Blazze Johnson is her first book.

blazze203
Instagram: authorgbj
Facebook: msgbjohnson
www.galebjohnson.com